Out of the Darkness, Into the Light

A Spiritual Journey

by
Heather Pinter

Dorrance Publishing Co
585 Alpha Drive
Suite 103
Pittsburgh, PA 15238
Visit our website at *www.dorrancebookstore.com*

ISBN: 978-1-6491-3177-5
eISBN: 978-1-6491-3702-9

Out of the Darkness, Into the Light

Dedicated to

The most precious gifts God has blessed me with, my boys, Koen Matthew and Isaiah Thomas; I was trusted with you, and nothing has given me more joy than to be called your mom.

And my Princess Jess, you may not have been born to me but will always be my daughter at heart.

Jeremiah 29:11-14

"For I know the plans I have for you," declares the Lord, "plans to prosper you and not to harm you, plans to give you a hope and a future. Then you will call upon me and come and pray to me, and I will listen to you. You will seek me and find me when you seek me with all your heart. I will be found by you," declares the Lord...

Contents

1971

Monday, March 15, 1971 at 9:48 A.M., to be exact. The exact same time my mom still calls me every year to wish her first born a Happy Birthday! I was the little, dark-haired baby girl my mom always dreamed she'd have. She named me Heather Angela Gaughran. I was the first grandchild on both sides and was spoiled, to say the least.

My dad was brought into the world on April 28, 1948. My grandma Ellen Gouldsmith named her baby boy Jerry Dean. She was a young, unwed mother, full of spark. She was working at the ice cream parlor on the Independence Square when Vince Gaughran caught her attention as he walked through the doors, all decked out in his navy uniform.

He must have been smitten as well because what led to a courtship eventually ended in marriage. Grandpa raised my dad as his own and Gram and Grandpa went on to have my Aunt Linda and Uncle John. My grandpa was an excellent carpenter and built the house from the ground up that they raised their family in.

My mom was born on September 19, 1952 to Harvey and Mary Lou Colston. My mom was named Mary Ann and was the youngest of three. She had an older sister Jamie and a brother Richard. When my mom was a young child, around three years old, my Grandma Colston had some mental health issues. This led to a very dysfunctional upbringing for my mom.

My mom was friends with my dad's sister, Linda, and that is how my parents met. My mom had a crush on my dad from the first time she saw him, and eventually, they started dating. My dad joined the army, and upon his return, they got married. My mom was young and eager to escape her home life and ready to put down some roots and start a family of her own. My mom had four kids in five years.

Carrie and I were only thirteen months apart. I was so jealous of her when she was just a baby that I was told that one time I walked across the room and held up a photo of her, tore it in half, laid it down, and continued to exit the room.

Another time, I crawled into her crib and bit her on the face. That was the beginning of a two-year biting spree. My mom couldn't take me anywhere. I actually drew blood on several occasions, including the gym nursery where my mom worked and at some friend's house that had twins that were about my age. My cousin Christine, who was a year older, was afraid to be around me. I'm sure glad I outgrew that phase!

Carrie and I were the best of friends after that (now that we're adults, we consider each other 'Sister Friends'). If Carrie fell down and scratched her knee on the sidewalk, I would pick her up and carry her in the house. She always looked up to me for protection.

I was four years old when Jessica was born. We were at my Grandma and Grandpa Gaughran's house when the call from the hospital came in that we had a sister. My comment was "another girl." I was so disappointed, because I wanted a brother (which I got a year later).

Jessi was always a bashful little girl. When she was in Kindergarten, she was too shy to raise her hand when the teacher called her name during roll call. She was always so sweet though and never far from my mom's side. That's why I feel so bad that even Jessi didn't get to escape my biting. I would fool her into a kiss on the cheek and then chomp down. I never drew blood but how mean! (I really did eventually outgrow the whole biting thing).

I was so happy when Brian was born. I finally got my brother. He was introduced to us girls as "your baby brother, Brian." He affectionately got the nickname BoBo when Jessi tried to say either "baby brother" or "Brian"; we're not sure which one. He's over 6' tall today, and I have to look up to him, but he'll always be my little brother.

Poor BoBo! Growing up with three older sisters must have been rough. Carrie and I would dress him up in this light blue dress and put baby powder in his hair (we always thought that's why he had blonde hair), and we called him Sally. Trust me when I say he paid us back when we got older. I can recall him chasing us around the back yard with a 2 x 4, probably well deserved.

We lived in a little house on Osage Trail in Independence, Missouri. My dad worked for Kansas City Power and Light, and my mom got to stay home and take care of us kids. I remember a lot of great things about growing up.

That's back in the day when Kindergarten was a half day, and I went in the morning. We had milk and cookies in class and learned our telephone number and how to count and the ABCs. Most of which is expected to be known in this day and age before entering elementary school. I also got to walk to and from school which I thought was cool. I thought I was such a big girl. I would round the corner to the other street and go through the school yard gate, and when I would make my way home, my mom would always be sitting on the front porch with a snack. I remember pecan sandies the most, because they were my favorite cookie.

Once, on my birthday, I was so proud carrying my cupcakes; I looked back at my mom, and I walked right into a tree. My mom recalls one second I was happy and the next second cupcakes were flying everywhere, and I was in tears! Luckily she made extra cupcakes. And another time I lost my tooth at school and carried it home in my stocking cap with two hands, careful not to drop it. In fact, I was so careful I was late getting home from school and had my mom in a panic.

Speaking of panic, that's the house that caught on fire. My mom was about six months pregnant with BoBo and was on the phone with her sister Jamie when she thought she smelled smoke. Carrie and I were watching *Sesame Street* and eating little sandwiches in fun shapes that my mom cut out for us. Sure enough, the electric fireplace in the basement sparked and caught fire.

As a mother myself, I can only imagine how frantic my mom must have felt trying to get her three small children out of a burning house. We didn't even have time to put our shoes on. I can remember going to the neighbor's house, crossing the snow-covered yard in bare feet. We stood looking out their front door as the fire truck pulled up to extinguish our little house. We had to live in an apartment until it was fixed up and ready to live in again.

We had some friends on the street too. I can remember Tommy lived up the street next to Charmin and her two sisters. I remember playing at their house and having lots of fun. We had a neighbor that would babysit sometimes. I took something from their house once, and my mom marched me straight back down there to return it. I never did that again. Then there were the Wagners that lived two houses from us to the left. They were a wild bunch of four boys.

I remember the first time I got to go to Worlds of Fun (Tickets were only $5 back then.), and John Wollschalger got to come with us. He was another neighbor that lived up the street. He was twelve years old, and I had a crush on him. My mom said I was boy crazy from the time I could walk.

Stan lived in the house on our right and liked to pick on me so much that my mom taught me how to fight. After I slugged him a few times, he left me alone. After that, we were the best of friends. All in all, I would say my memories on Osage Trail were pretty happy ones!

1978

I **was seven years old when my parents split up. If you want to** know the truth, I don't think divorce affected me like most kids. I felt a sense of relief. I love my dad and can honestly say as an adult, our relationship is good. But when I was young, he wasn't always very pleasant to be around. My parents fought a lot and were in an unhappy marriage that resulted in divorce.

By this time, we no longer lived in our "little" house on Osage Trail but instead what we called the "big" house on Buckner Tarsney Road in Buckner, Missouri. It was a much larger home that sat on an acre out in the country.

Some say it was haunted. Just ask my Aunt Jamie who encountered some supernatural experiences when she would babysit. She swears up and down that she heard someone knocking on the door, and when she opened it, nobody was there. That happened to her more than once. And there was the time there were footprints in the snow that went all the way around the house but didn't go anywhere. Pretty weird, huh?

Carrie and I slept upstairs, and we always felt a strange, creepy presence in the room. One night, Carrie actually felt a hand push her back in bed. Needless to say, we didn't like bedtime in that house.

We had a really big tree house out there that was a lot of fun to play in. The yard was huge, and we would run and play outside all day. That was back when kids wanted to play outside. We didn't have all the distractions that we have today with electronic devices and social media and such.

That's where I learned how to ride my minibike. I would circle that thing round n' round that big yard, until one day, I ran smack dab into the privacy fence by the barrel that my dad would burn trash in. I just lost control. I remember smacking my lip and bruising my knee, and I didn't ever want to ride that thing again. I think maybe my ego was a little bruised too.

Carrie and I would walk up to the little general store and purchase candy and bubble gum for a nickel. Boy, those really were the good ol' days for me. Just a much simpler time with not as much to worry about.

This is the house I broke my nose in. I got roller skates that year for Christmas. We would put music on our record player and skate around the poles that supported the ceiling. The floors were easy for skating, and one day, my two-year-old brother was straddling the pole, and I tripped over him and landed face first on the cold cement floor.

My mom heard screaming and hurried to the basement to see what was going on. She met me on the stairs and rushed me to the bathroom. I can remember the sink filling up with blood; so much blood. We went to the hospital, but there wasn't much that could be done for a broken nose. When I went back to school, I was embarrassed, because I had two black eyes.

I was seven years old when my parents got divorced. That same year my mom married Jim Bailey, and we moved to Blue Springs, Missouri. We lived in a duplex on Sunset and life seemed pretty good. He was a really fun guy. He managed the bowling alley, so we spent a lot of time there. I enjoyed it. I learned how to bowl and got on a bowling league.

Every other weekend we would spend time with our dad. That mostly meant we spent a lot of time at his parent's house, because that's where he was staying. I can't begin to tell you just how much that time in my life came to mean to me as an adult. My Grandma and Grandpa Gaughran were a huge influence in my life from very early on. I don't mention my maternal grandparents much, because I didn't really know them very well.

My grandpa was a navy man, so he was a little gruff. My mom told me after I was born, grandpa softened up. In fact, I was given the name "Heather" because my grandpa liked it. My grandparents said if they would have had another girl, they would have named her Heather.

They would come pick me up when we lived on Osage Trail, and I would be waiting out on the front porch with my little suitcase packed for overnight. As a toddler, I would stand between them in the truck, way before car seats were a thing, and tickle my grandpa's ear. I'm pretty sure I had him wrapped around my little finger, and he didn't even know it. He called me his "little Heather."

Grandpa had a shop in his garage where he would make airplane wings as a hobby. I'm still not sure what he used them for, but we always had to save our popsicle sticks for him. I always thought they were to spread glue with. Gram would have to keep us kids quiet or else Grandpa would holler up the stairs "Keep it down!"

My gram was everything to me. Being the oldest, I always wanted to be part of the adults. I would never say anything, just listen. Gram was a bit of a gossip, and every Saturday morning Mary and Linda, my great aunts, would come have coffee with us, and I always had to be a part of the conversation. They always had the scoop on what was going on in the family.

Eventually my dad married Susie. She had two kids, Tina and Kenny, and we all got along really well. We would take family trips to the lake together and things like that. I remained close to my grandparents throughout the years.

1983

By the time I was twelve years old, I felt socially awkward. When I was in sixth grade (that was still considered elementary school) some of the kids called me Dolly Parton, if you can guess why. I developed at an early age; what can I say?

That's the year I met my best friend Dawn. We're still friends today. She was my partner in crime. My family moved to a duplex on Westminister. Dawn lived a few houses up the street, and we were in the same sixth grade class. We were inseparable all through our middle and high school years. I used to go to Dawn's, because I had a crush on her older brother, and that's where I could smoke cigarettes. That's back when you could buy a pack for $1.35.

One time I thought I was sneaking up there only to find my pack of cigarettes were missing. Come to find out, Carrie stuffed them in the farthest coat pocket in the closet after circling the Surgeon General's warning with black sharpie. I was so mad! I guess she was protective of me too. She didn't like the fact that I was smoking.

The summer between sixth and seventh grade I had to have foot surgery to remove my bunions on both feet. I got bunions at such an early age because of the way my feet naturally angle when I stand. I have to wear custom foot supports for the rest of my life. It's a good thing my job requires good comfortable shoes.

I believe my foot problems played a part in contributing to my lack of self-esteem. It kept me from being able to run because of the pain. And when we had to go swimming in elementary school, I was so embarrassed, I tried to hide my feet. After the surgery, I had casts on both feet. I had to learn how to walk all over again with a walker and crutches. My mom got to stay with me in the hospital and sleep on a cot.

When I came home, there was quite a bit of recovery. I had to sleep with my feet elevated every night. Once I started seventh grade, I had to wear these hideous wooden shoes, and to make matters worse, every Thursday the school bus would stop in front of my doctor's office. How embarrassing. It just made me really self-conscious.

By this time my mom and Jim were getting a divorce. Little did my mom know that before she met Jim, he was addicted to drugs. While they were married he got back into some things that she didn't want around her four babies, so he had to go. My mom didn't mess around!

My mom was a single mother of four kids and had to work two jobs without a car. Luckily, she didn't have to go without a car for very long, but I still don't know how she did it. We always had a roof over our heads. We didn't have much else, but we had each other. I would say we were considered poor monetarily.

Sometimes, the church would bring us boxes of food and clothes. I can remember putting the food on the shelf and how the clothes smelled like moth balls. But we were rich in so many other ways. There were times we ate popcorn for dinner. We just thought we were lucky.

We grew up going to church. My cousin Christine spent a lot of time with us in the summer when we went to church camp. We loved sitting around the campfire and singing songs. I got baptized in a swimming pool at church camp when I was eight years old. That's a day I'll never forget.

We celebrated birthday parties with streamers and balloons and homemade cakes that my mom would decorate. She's always had a knack with creativity.

And we would have a costume party for Halloween. She would make a pumpkin piñatas with papier-mâché (strips of newspaper dipped in flour water). She would fill it with candy for us and our friends to take a swing at.

Every year she would let us each have a friend over for a Thanksgiving feast, and we would all take turns saying what we were thankful for.

At Christmas, Mom made sure we knew the "reason for the season." The birth of our Savior, Jesus Christ. All the gifts were in honor of Him. Us kids would hold a little empty, wrapped box and place it under the tree for Jesus. What we put inside were things from our heart like love, hope, joy, and kindness. Years later, my mom would bake a cake for Jesus and let her grandkids decorate it. We had a lot of wonderful traditions!

But as the years grew on, I got more and more rebellious. I really gave my mom a hard time as a teenager. I wanted to do my own thing. I didn't think any rules applied to me. I was a poor student. I skipped a lot of school. I got in fights and spent time in detention. I was a little promiscuous. My mom found hickies on my neck and cigarettes in my drawer.

I was very angry and didn't know exactly why. Maybe it was the lack of my own father in my life. He'd get us kids on weekends, but I can remember some lapses in visits at times. And I know he wasn't consistent on child support which was a real hardship on my mom.

I did manage to get and hold a job when I was fifteen at V's Pasta Parlor at the Independence Center. I learned a lot and took pride in that job. I worked myself up to assistant manager. I got to fire somebody once. I thought that was neat. That's the job where I learned the phrase "If you have time to lean, you have time to clean!" I liked having my own money too.

But at seventeen years old, my personal life was a complete mess, and Jesus was nowhere on the horizon.

1988

Shawn was three years older than me, and I really thought that he was something. From the first time I saw him, he had that "bad boy" persona. He had long hair that he meticulously combed and beautiful blue eyes. But he was definitely a bad influence on me. He didn't care that I was a student or that I had rules and a curfew. He did care that I had a job and a car, two things he didn't have.

I ended up leaving home and moving in with Shawn and his alcoholic mom and her husband, because I didn't like my mom's rules such as "get up and go to school." They lived in Oak Grove in a trailer out in the country. My parents put their heads together and thought that if they took my car away from me that I would come home. It didn't matter. I was so stubborn that I would sometimes hitchhike to work. I mean, how crazy! Looking back, it amazes me some of the things I did. Carrie would come out and pick me up on Saturday mornings, because we both worked at the mall.

I eventually dropped out of school but got my GED with the support of my dad. The living conditions were really bad at Shawn's. Did I mention his mom was an alcoholic? She would get drunk and was extremely jealous of me. She actually thought I was trying to steal her husband. He was a truck driver, so he would be gone for extended days at a time, but when he was home, I couldn't walk across the living room to use the bathroom, because she would accuse me of attracting his attention, so I would have to stick my hiney out the bedroom window to pee. How humiliating!

I used to go to Planned Parenthood for birth control but stopped taking it for some reason. I think I lost them in the move. Once I found out I was pregnant, it was like I grew up overnight. I knew this wasn't a good environment for my baby. I could have gone back home with my mom, but Carrie was pregnant with Courtney at the time, and I didn't want to impose. That's when I moved in with my grandparents. They didn't hesitate to open their doors to me. I lived with them during my whole pregnancy and the next year after.

They gave me a bedroom, and I set it up with my bed and dresser on one side and a baby crib on the other. I had a Mickey and Minnie Mouse theme. There was a little couch and rocking chair (for when the baby was born) and a TV set up in there too. My gram used to say I was the best house guest, because I kept to myself and cleaned up all my messes. She never even noticed I was there.

I got a job in Blue Springs at Price Chopper in the deli. My grandparents lived in Independence, and when my car bit the dust, they would drive me back and forth to work. They never once complained. They never even suggested I find something closer, they just did it.

They were always there for me. They were the best thing in my life at the time, and I learned so much from them. Their marriage was the epitome of marriage to me. I wanted what they had, and I wanted to someday be the wife that my gram was. She was patient, loving, kind, funny, and so much more. I literally never saw her mad. She was my role model and my confidant.

Years later, when I sat with my precious gram in the hospital just a couple of weeks before she passed away, we reminisced about everything. There was nothing left unsaid between us. She told me that she needed me and my baby every bit as much as we needed her; that she was lonely, and we gave her purpose at that particular time in her life. We gave her purpose? How ironic!

1990

It was a Thursday afternoon, and I just got finished deep cleaning the house and sat down on the couch with a glass of iced tea. I suppose I was "nesting" and didn't even realize it at the time, because my due date wasn't for another week. Gram was at her weekly visit with her mom. Every Thursday was her TOPS day. She and her sisters would go to Club in the morning and then go out to lunch and then spend the rest of the day visiting Ma (my great-grandma). Ma lived right behind Gram, so all we had to do was cut through the back yard and we were there.

As soon as I sat down and relaxed, I felt my first contraction. Several hours later, Gram took me to Truman Medical Center East. Shawn met us there. I remember lying on this hard examination table but never being admitted. It felt like we were there for hours until they told me to come back when my contractions were closer together. I went home with my mom and stayed up all night in labor.

At noon the next day, June 22nd, we went back to the hospital. This time they admitted me. My whole family was waiting patiently in the waiting room. They didn't determine the sex back then, so I didn't know if I was going to have a boy or a girl.

A funny story I like to tell people is when my "son" was born the delivery nurse said, "It's a girl. No wait; it's a boy." You can imagine the thought I must have had at first thinking I had a daughter then a son!

I already had his name picked out. Koen Matthew Gaughran. Gaughran was my maiden name. He was born on June 22, 1990 at 4:05 P.M. He had a perfectly shaped, tiny, round head and chubby little cheeks. He was so sweet.

It was difficult at first though, because when the nurses first sent me home from the hospital, my water had actually already broken which caused an infection. My brand-new baby had to stay in the hospital for a week after he was born, because they didn't want the infection to spread to him. His poor little thighs looked like pincushions because of all the times they had to prick them.

I wanted to breastfeed him so either my mom or my gram would drive me to the hospital for every feeding. When it was time to bring Koen home, my mom went with me to the hospital, with a car seat in tow. What a glorious day indeed!

About six weeks after Koen was born, I bought a new car. I drove a 1990 red Nissan Sentra off the lot. I was so proud. I decided to report it to the Division of Family Services, because I considered myself to be a fairly honest person. I was getting some financial help from the state, and when I reported that I got a car, thinking I was doing the right thing, they terminated my welfare. They said if I could afford a car payment then I didn't need assistance from the state.

Where's the justice in that? A young, single mom, unable to get any help from the state just because she has a car payment. I was trying to better myself, but that's okay. It just made me stronger, and I worked harder. I did qualify for the WIC (women infant children) program that provided grocery items such as juice, milk, cheese, cereal, and baby formula. It was a great blessing.

My gram was Koen's primary caregiver. She watched him every day of the week except on Thursday, her Club day. My manager at Price Chopper was flexible with my schedule, so I always had Thursdays off.

Koen was a sickly child. I always contributed his health issues to our experience in the hospital when he was born. He got pneumonia at six months old and was diagnosed with asthma at an early age. I'm so thankful that my baby was in such good hands with Gram. She was known as Mee-Ma to all of her great grandkids.

By now my relationship with Shawn was strained, to say the least. It never was considered healthy, but it got pretty bad. Shawn was a drug addict and a thief. He would use IV drugs and go on binges where he would take my car for days, burglarizing people's houses, and bringing hot stuff home to turn around and trade for the little white stuff.

He would also break into people's cars. I remember, on more than one occasion, before Koen was born, hunkering down in the back seat, waiting for Shawn to return after going on a stealing spree. I don't know what else you call it. I was put in dangerous situations with him all the time. I'm surprised I lived to talk about it.

Another time he wanted me to know what it was like to sneak around someone's house, lurking in the windows. The homeowners must have seen our shadows, because all of a sudden, the back door flew open and this man yelled at us. Shawn grabbed me by the hand, and we bolted. All I can remember is being dragged through backyards, left wondering what just happened.

When Koen was seven months old, Shawn went to jail for 120 days. Every week on my day off I would drive to the Corrections Facility in Cameron, Missouri. He swore up and down he had changed, and I wanted to believe that. I really wanted that for him and us. He did his time and got released right before Koen's first birthday.

We rented a little place a block from my Gram's. I loved that house. It wasn't much, but it was mine. It didn't take long for Shawn to quit his job and relapse. Pretty soon he was gone at night bringing more stolen stuff in the house. I was scared for the safety of me and my baby. Not only that, I refused to support him and his lifestyle.

I made the decision to move in with my dad and Kathy, and they accepted Koen and I with open arms. Dad and Susie's marriage didn't work out, and they got divorced a few years earlier. Kathy has always been an asset to our family and a great fit for my dad. They lived in an earth contact home in Lone Jack, Missouri. My dad fixed the whole upstairs into a little apartment for Koen and me.

I would get up every morning and take Koen to my grandparents. I would take him from the car and put him directly in bed with Gram and then go into the kitchen and tell Grandpa good morning and grab a bagel.

My dad kept Koen on Thursdays, and it was good for them. He owned property in Napoleon (North of Oak Grove), where he and Kathy would eventually live. Koen would go with him each week, and they would always stop at Casey's for a donut.

Even though I was living with my dad and Gram kept Koen when I worked, I still saw Shawn. By this time, he and his mother and step dad were living in Independence. I tried to break up with him over and over, but he was so controlling it was ridiculous.

He would get so jealous that if I was a few minutes late, he would search my body looking for any sign, like a hickey, that I was with somebody else. Or he would tear my wallet apart looking for a phone number that never existed.

I couldn't even go to the swimming pool, because he couldn't handle the thought of someone else looking at me. This was before cell phones, so I can only imagine how he would have gone through my recent call list or text messages, etc.

And then there were the times he would literally keep me up all night. He would force me to stay awake, and then I would have to go to work the next day. A lot of psychological mind games were played.

I know you're probably wondering why I stayed with him for so long (six and a half years). I'll admit it was a very dysfunctional, codependent relationship. The tip of the iceberg for me though was Christmas Eve 1994. Shawn had been to court due to some probation violations and some other broken laws of some kind. I can't remember the specifics anymore, but he was supposed to turn himself in the day after Christmas. The courts were trying to be nice and let him spend Christmas with his family before jail time. So, Koen and I were with him for this last night together, and the next thing I know, my car was gone. He literally stole my car, and what makes matters worse, he left me stranded with his drunk mother on Christmas Eve.

Of course, he would rather be out getting his last fix before jail instead of spending time with his family. Somehow her and I ended up in a scuffle, and she reached up with both hands and grabbed my four-year-old son by the hair and yanked him down. My adrenaline kicked in, and I slugged the woman in the eye. I found out a few days later that I gave her a black eye. All I can say is don't mess with Mama Bear.

I called my mom at 3:00 A.M. to come pick us up. When she got there, Koen and I were standing out in the snow with Christmas presents from Santa in tow. Shawn called me the next day and told me where my car was. This stint in jail was the perfect time for me to move on.

I was working at Foster's Dry Cleaners in Blue Springs. My manager had been trying to set me up with her sister's ex-husband, Joe. She said he was a really nice guy, so I agreed.

1995

Joe was the total opposite from Shawn. He had a job and a house and a truck. He seemed normal. He even had a DVD player, caller ID, house plants, and a dog named Shalimar. He was a contributing member of society. He was also fifteen years my senior, but I didn't care. Age never mattered to us. Joe was my knight in shining armor, and he swooped in on a white horse. He was my everything!

Joe called me on January 5th, and we talked for two hours. I remember I laughed a lot; he was so funny. He lived in Bonner Springs, Kansas, and on Saturday, January 7th, he drove all the way out to Lone Jack to meet me in person, and that was all she wrote. He had me at hello. He had thick, dark hair, beautiful green eyes, and a wonderful smile. He came in and met my dad and Kathy, and they immediately loved him. I don't think Joe's ever met a stranger. Koen even seemed to like Joe. All went well that first day.

He drove Koen and I back to his house, and on the way there, he asked Koen for permission to hold my hand. He seemed like a perfect gentleman. When we were standing in his living room, he kissed me. I was awestruck!

Joe wanted to take me to his place of employment, so he could give me a tour of the warehouse and his office. There was a photo of a woman sitting on his desk. It was one of those "Glamour Shots" in a frame. He turned it over, face down on his desk, and carried on as if he didn't just deliberately turn this picture frame over. Just like when I was a little girl and I tore my sister's photo in half, as if she didn't matter. I should have questioned it at the time, but I didn't. Remember, I was smitten, but it should have been a red flag.

I had prearranged for Koen to spend the night at a friend's house, so after we dropped him off, we went to a Chinese restaurant. He then drove me home and came inside for a bit. He lay me on the floor, face down, and gave me a back rub. Then he went home. I literally thought I just met my Prince Charming!

I can remember having Joe come back out there for dinner a couple days later. I was trying to impress him, and because my dad and Kathy had venison in the freezer, venison it was. It went over pretty well. And then the very next day I drove to his place, and he prepared butterfly pork chops on the grill with steamed green beans and au gratin potatoes. It was magical. He was so interested in me and getting to know me. He drew me in, and he seemed to really like my son.

I would never recommend what we did next. I moved in with Joe literally one week after meeting him. I don't even know how it happened, because I don't remember ever having a conversation about it. All of a sudden, we were loading all of my possessions in the back of his truck, and my family was actually on board. But considering the relationship I just came out of with Shawn, Joe looked pretty good, so no one questioned how fast things were moving, and I was a twenty-three-year-old girl that embraced it. For the first time in my life, this quality person just seemed to show up out of nowhere, right when I needed him most. He just took me in and not only me, my four-and-a-half-year-old son. Who does that?

Shortly after that, he set me up with an appointment for new glasses and took me to his dentist. Things seemed really good at first. He would leave me love notes and buy me cards and flowers. He suggested finding a church. We would take Jerimie, Joe's eleven-year-old son from a previous marriage, on the weekends with us. Church didn't last long, but we made an effort right from the beginning. He really seemed like a very affectionate, loving family man.

He also made a point to tell me that he never said "I love you," in which I responded, "Okay." But it wasn't okay, and I didn't know that at the time. I didn't know that someday that twenty-three-year-old girl would grow up and have an ache in her heart for those three very simple, important words. Another red flag.

Shortly after, there seemed to be a cool distance between us. It didn't help that Koen was having crying spells at night. He was only four years old at the time. This was a big adjustment for him. He was always a bit of a mama's boy, but that's because I felt very protective of him where his biological father was concerned.

Anyway, remember the photo of the girl in his office? Well, she manifested. I found out he had been sneaking around and seeing her behind my back. I mean, I realize I was young and naïve, but I thought living with him automatically made me his girlfriend, but Joe had a hard time with commitment. This went on until I moved out eight months later.

It was a good thing for me to get out on my own. Gram was still watching Koen, and I was still working at Foster's Dry Cleaners. We were living in SunnySide Garden Apartments in Blue Springs. I was still talking to Joe and dating him some, but I knew he was still seeing the other woman.

He was supposed to spend Christmas Eve with me that year, but he never showed up. I waited all night. On Christmas morning, I heard a knock at the door. It was Joe, bright eyed and bushy tailed, like he didn't just stand me up. Another red flag.

That's a classic sign of NPD. They take advantage of others to get what they want. That's why he thought he could just waltz back in with no explanation. There's something I've learned over the years and that is we teach people how to treat us. I never should have let him in.

By the time Koen was five years old, he was extremely involved with children's theater. I would take him to auditions and rehearsals and performances from the time he was age five to fifteen. He loved it. I ended up getting involved with running the sound booth that spring, so Koen and I were kept pretty busy. I was beginning to move on with my life.

Once Joe thought he was losing me for good, he did something I never expected. He went out and bought a ring and proposed. He asked me to marry him in public, right there in front of my family at one of Koen's performances. I said yes, of course.

I moved out of my apartment in Blue Springs and back in with him in Bonner Springs. By this time, Koen was in Kindergarten, and I got a job in Kansas City, Kansas as an administrative assistant in a small business office called Trans 300, Inc.

I spent the next two years trying to get him to commit to a wedding day. He always got agitated. Looking back, it was clear he was putting it off. I couldn't understand why. Still to this day, he will tell people that I forced him into marriage. But yet he's the one that asked me. I just genuinely loved Joe and wanted to be his wife. I knew some things were a little bit off, but nothing is perfect, right? I think even back then I thought maybe marriage would fix Joe. Maybe then he could trust me with his heart. I can tell you now, I spent the next twenty-one years trying.

1998

The latter part of 1997, Joe and I bought a house from my Aunt Linda and Uncle Gary. It was in Independence, Missouri at 612 W 24th Street and couldn't have been better timing. We fixed it up, and I guess Joe was on such a high from that, that he decided it was time to set a wedding date. He didn't have to tell me twice.

We were attending Stony Point Christian Church at the time in Kansas City, Kansas. I called them to set a date before he could change his mind. The next available date was March 7th, so I booked it. My mom and I threw together a quick wedding, and it was fabulous. It was a fairytale wedding in my eyes. We had it at our church with a traditional cake and punch reception. All of our friends and family were there. It was white and purple, just lovely.

My mom has always been my biggest fan. She stayed up until midnight the night before my wedding day writing me a beautiful poem:

Thoughts of you keep pouring through my mind,
As I lay here in bed trying to unwind.
Thinking of you when you were just a baby,
And how you've become such a beautiful lady.

When you were first born I was a little uptight,
I worried about doing everything just right.
But from the way you've turned out to be,
God surely must have been watching over me.

I remember when you used to bite.
It really was a terrible sight.
And the time you slipped and bit your lip.
Girl, life with you was really a trip.

When you were two you cut yourself with a knife.
When you were six you wrecked the mini bike.
When you were seven you broke your nose.
You really knew how to keep me on my toes.

And speaking of toes, I'd like to mention,
When you were twelve you had your foot operation.
I stayed in your room overnight,
Because you didn't want me out of your sight.

And then you went to Junior High;
My patience you really wanted to try.
You liked to fight; you were pretty tough,
But you were just my angel in the rough.

I guess what I'm really trying to say,
As I watched you growing from day to day,
I've been with you through thick and thin,
And now it's time for your new life to begin.

And it's really hard for me to let go,
Although deep inside I honestly know,

This is the happiest time of your life,
To finally become Joe Pinter's Wife!

Joe surprised me with a rented Cadillac. It was decorated with cans and the words "Just Married" written across the window. We had the most amazing honeymoon. We went to Hanibal, Missouri and stayed in a bed-and-breakfast. That was my first time in a B&B and I've had a love for them ever since. I can remember Joe and I sitting on the bed and tossing all the money we got from the wedding up in the air and rolling around in it.

I realized later that when I threw away all the envelopes that the cards and cash came in that I accidently threw out our marriage certificate. I was upset at first, but it worked out okay. All I had to do was request another one. I was so happy to be Mrs. Joe Pinter!

Right after we were married, I found out I was expecting another baby. Koen was so excited to be a big brother. Joe had two sons, Joseph and Jerimie, from his previous marriage, so we all wanted a girl, but God had a different plan in mind.

On November 20, 1998, Isaiah Thomas Pinter graced us with his presence. He was absolutely perfect, and by then, it didn't matter if we had a boy or a girl, just as long as our baby was healthy. Life seemed great the first year. Having a baby together seemed like exactly what we needed.

I was able to quit my job at Trans 300, Inc. after Isaiah was born. I loved staying home and really enjoyed being a housewife and took great pride in it. I was able to send Koen off to school and be there for his return. I kept the house clean, the laundry washed, and hot meals on the table. Life was good. If Joe was late, he always had a plate waiting for him in the microwave. And I never complained about his long hours or my job at home. I was just thankful for a man that took care of his family and that I had a washing machine to wash clothes and a kitchen to cook meals.

Joe worked for the Lee Apparel Co. as Supervisor of Facilities Monday through Friday. He stayed busy on the weekends with side jobs, and eventually, he had three rental homes. He's a handy man by trade and a great one at that. Joe has always been a very hard worker. That's one of the things that drew me to him. He doesn't have a lazy bone in his body. It's also how he defines himself. That was actually his way of loving me, by providing for his wife and kids. The problem with that is there was no emotion involved, no affection in any way. Just the way Joe liked it. People with NPD have a hard time bonding with people, even their spouse. I was content for a long time, but eventually, it took a toll on me.

That first year seemed to fly by, and on our first wedding anniversary, my mom stayed overnight with the boys so Joe and I could get away. After dinner, we went back to our hotel room, and I had this cute little silky, lavender lingerie set that I so proudly adorned. I mean, here I was a young wife trying to appeal to my husband on what was a very special night, right?

I'm sharing this with you, because it sets the course of my intimate relationship with my husband. I remember it so vividly; Joe was sitting on a chair in the corner, and I expected him to respond to me affectionately, to reciprocate my actions. But instead, he proceeds to tell me that I'm not very good in bed.

I know that a symptom of NPD is to have an inability or unwillingness to recognize the needs and feelings of others and to belittle them. But I did not know that at the time. I was humiliated. I don't know how else to describe it. I was stunned, speechless, and a little piece of me died in that room. I don't even remember how the night ended, if we made love or not. But I remember the scars it left on me that day. I struggled on whether or not to share such a personal detail but ultimately thought it was important to establish the intimacy that was lost so early on in my marriage and the shame that came with it.

All through the years of my marriage, I felt insecure about my role in the bedroom. When I should have been nurtured and loved, I felt rejected and ashamed with the one person who should have cared the most.

I continued to love Joe wholeheartedly. I gave 110 percent to make up for my shortcomings. I always had to work double time to try to be seen by Joe. I don't think he ever really noticed me, but I never gave up trying.

2000

This was the year I forced myself to throw up in the toilet for the first time. I was always self-conscious about my weight, but more than that, it was an emotion that I thought I could control. I enjoyed eating, and I found comfort in food. I could eat as much as I wanted and didn't have to keep it down. Binge and purge. Binge and purge. I knew there was a name for it. Bulimia Nervosa. But I never really admitted it to myself. It was just a dirty little secret, one that I carried around for years, until now.

Bulimia nervosa is an eating disorder that's described as a destructive pattern of eating and purging to control weight (or taking an overabundance of laxatives). Unlike anorexia nervosa, bulimia doesn't have symptoms of weight loss, but the effects are still very real. Two behaviors of bulimia are binging (eating a lot of food) and purging (self-induced vomiting).

For some people, bulimia can encompass so much more than that. It can take a tremendous emotional toll. For example, it's possible to experience obsessive-compulsive behaviors, depression, anxiety, and constant monitoring of food and weight can become an obsession.

I never really took it that serious. Maybe I should have. I was just always more concerned about everybody else in my life. I never related my OCD to bulimia, but I guess it was a way of being in control of something. I didn't consider my disorder hardcore, but it was there, nonetheless.

I went to Slim 4 Life and lost a significant amount of weight in 2002 but once I reached my goal, I was back on the hamster wheel, spinning out of control. A real serious roller coaster ride of emotions. Always feeling inadequate, never measuring up. It was just how I learned how to deal with things, in private, on my own.

Joe always talked about adopting Koen after we got married. I can remember how excited Koen was at the prospect of having a dad. Shawn was an absent father which I always thought was for the best. He was in prison again at the time, so our attorney mailed him the adoption papers, but he refused to sign them. It just ended up costing us more time and money.

Gram and Grandpa loved Joe from the beginning. They were so excited for Koen to be adopted that Gram gave me five hundred dollars to go towards the attorney fee. After it was final, we had a big adoption party with family and friends. It was great.

Koen won an essay at school about his new dad. He got to treat his class to Krispy Kreme Donuts, and we got to go to the Royals game and meet Slugger. It was really fun.

Several years later, the relationship between Joe and Koen was tarnished. As Koen got older, he could see through Joe. NPD comes with a wide range of signs and symptoms. Sometimes Joe would become impatient or angry and react with rage or contempt, because he had a difficult time regulating emotions and behavior.

Then there was the side of him the rest of the world got to see. The charismatic, charming, fun-loving, perfect side of Joe. I've often told him "that's the Joe I love the most." Sadly, he can't maintain that character trait. With Joe, I experienced extreme mood swings. It left a bad taste in Koen's mouth, and he found it to be hypocritical.

I always made excuses for Joe. I felt a real need to love him even harder. I just remember thanking God every day for the blessings in my life. I always felt like I owed Joe in some way for swooping in and taking care of Koen and I, and I learned how to love and accept Joe for who he was, flaws and all.

In 2003 we moved from 24th Street to Sioux Court. It was what they call an atrium split. It was a beautiful home, and I loved it. I had been involved with direct sales through Pampered Chef for about four or five years at this point. It was a good income for me. I became a director which meant I had consultants under me, and it came along with a little more money. I enjoyed it. It got me out of the house a couple nights a week and gave me a social circle.

We ended up transferring our church membership to First Baptist Church of Raytown. It was a huge church but much closer to home. We really liked it. We attended church every week, and Isaiah was involved in the Awanas program. We joined a Sunday school class and got connected. Joe and I would volunteer in the nursery as well. It was there that myself, Joe and Koen rededicated our life to Christ through baptism.

It was during our time at FBR that we met an elderly couple that were foster parents. I thought this is what we really needed, another baby in the house. Joe agreed, and we started classes. It was pretty detailed; they did a home study and we got certified.

All we had to do now was wait.

2005

It was August 26, 2005 when we got the call. Our social worker wanted to place an infant baby girl with us. All we were told was that her mom was incarcerated when she delivered her six weeks premature, and she was ready to come out of NICU and needed a home. Our social worker wanted to know if we could come to the hospital to meet the baby before we brought her home the next day. I already had a Pampered Chef Party scheduled that I couldn't cancel at such short notice.

Joe gladly accepted and still gets tears in his eyes when he talks about holding her for the first time. He spent an hour bonding with that sweet baby girl. He gave her a bottle and rocked her before kissing her goodbye and telling her we'd be back in the morning to take her home with us.

The next morning, we loaded up the car seat and headed to the hospital. We met the social worker there and signed the necessary documents declaring us her official guardians.

She already had the name Jess. Simply and beautifully, Jess. We absolutely loved and adored her. Joe and I had placed a crib in our bedroom right next to the rocking chair. I can distinctly remember getting up through the night for her bottle feedings.

When we brought Jess home, Koen had just turned fifteen, and Isaiah was six. They loved her as a sister from the very beginning. I used to bathe her in my bathroom sink, and Isaiah loved to help. I would get the kids off to school and spend the day being Jess's mom.

Things seemed perfect; Joe was so happy. We were there for all her milestones, rolling over, crawling, solid foods, etc. When Jess was three months old, I had to take her in for a paternity test. They needed to determine who her father was. To be honest, we didn't want to know who her father was because we wanted her to be ours. We got into fostering because we really had hoped to eventually adopt.

We were already in love with Jess, so how perfect would that have been for us to get to keep her? But once again, God had other plans. A few weeks later, the test results came back, and they confirmed Danny as her father.

From that point on I would take Jess to DFS each week for supervised visits with her biological father. I tried not to like Danny, because I knew that eventually we would lose Jess to him. But he was always prompt for his visits, and he always complied with the courts. It was clear from the beginning that he wanted to have custody of his daughter, and we knew as foster parents it was our job to provide the best home for her that we could, but the end result was always reunification.

That year flew by. We didn't really know exactly how much time we were going to have with Jess, so we made a point to enjoy every moment we had with her. Danny's visits went from supervised to unsupervised that eventually progressed into overnight stays.

That's the year we moved from Sioux Ct to Hanthorn Dr. Jess was nine months old at the time. We just wanted to downsize and get away from all the stairs in the atrium split to a raised ranch style home. There was already a bedroom with pink wallpaper and a big, front window just perfect for her. I used to rock Jess and sing to her every day in front of that window.

Jess' birthday is July 10th. That year we celebrated her first birthday on the fourth of July. We had a patriotic cake and ice cream with presents. Carrie and her husband hosted, because it was a holiday, and they had a swimming pool, so friends and family were already due to be there. We invited Danny and he got to attend.

A mere two days later, on July 6th, just four days before her official birthday, we had to say goodbye. It was heartbreaking for the whole family. Packing her little suitcase and waiting for Danny to come pick her up for the last time was one of the hardest things we ever had to do. It was hard on her too. We were the only family she knew up to that point.

We knew without a shadow of a doubt that we gave Jess the best possible first year of her life, but her absence left such a void that it honestly felt like we were mourning a death. It left a hole in our hearts. That's when a real distance was set in between Joe and me. You see, we mourned differently. It was at that time when I really needed my husband the most, but Joe doesn't deal with emotion and this was certainly no different. He did what he always does. He pushed all those feelings down and didn't want to deal with them. He built those walls so high around him that nobody was getting in, especially me. It put a real strain on our marriage, to put it mildly.

Not long after, we were placed with another little girl. Her name was Chevelle, Chevy for short. We loved her too, but it just wasn't the same for me. I missed my sweet baby Jess! I couldn't accept that she was gone, so I managed to work out a little something with Danny. He agreed that I could pick Jess up on Wednesdays and then return her on Thursday. That arrangement went on for a few months, then something changed with his schedule, and he needed a babysitter, so for the latter part of 2005, I would go to the home he shared with his girlfriend and watch Jess three days a week.

I would find myself doing Jess's laundry, tidying the house, and even cooking dinner so Danny would have a hot meal to come home to. Over the next couple months, Danny and I grew closer. I knew it was wrong, but it felt really good to be appreciated. Somebody was taking notice of me. One of Satan's ploys. He knew what strings to pull, and I fell right into his trap.

2007

This is the part of the story where guilt takes root. Sometimes the truth hurts, and I don't want to hurt anybody in any way, but I can't truly tell my story and leave this next part out. I'm not trying to justify it, but Joe knew exactly how much time I was spending with Jess's dad and never seemed to have a care in the world. I know it wasn't right, but I remember thinking "Joe really must not care about me at all if he can see me getting close to another man and do nothing to stop me." In fact, Danny's the person who taught me how to text, and I would sit right there in front of my husband while texting another man.

I was definitely seeking attention from Danny, and it eventually caught up with us. We gave in to our desires, so to speak, and fell into sin. Satan is in the business to steal, kill, and destroy, and I was no exception. I wasn't equipped to fight this spiritual warfare and gave in to my temptation. Satan knows all of our weaknesses and seeps into the cracks of our lives with only one agenda, to destroy all that falls prey. He already knew my marriage was flimsy at best. By now, after nine years of marriage, I was starting to feel the effects of the lack of love and intimacy that I so longed for. I'm ashamed to say that I found it in the arms of another man.

This lasted a few months before Joe caught wind of my indiscretions. There was definite turmoil. I thought Joe simply wouldn't care, but that couldn't have been farther from the truth. At first he was mad, naturally. He called Danny's live-in girlfriend and got her involved. She kicked him out, so he had to move. My kids got involved. It was a mess!

After Joe simmered down, he tried to make it up to me. I'd never seen him that way before, ever. He told me he was sorry for not being there for me when I needed him the most and for being a lousy husband. He bent over backwards trying to make amends, even telling me that he couldn't live without me. But instead of embracing this new revelation, it made me angry. I wanted to know why it took something like me having an affair to make him realize that. Now all of a sudden he loves me, and he cares about me. Why now?

Right in the midst of all this, our license with the state required another two-year commitment if we wanted to remain foster parents. I simply couldn't do it, so we had to say goodbye to Chevy, and she got placed in another home. I felt really bad, but in light of all of our personal problems at the time, I didn't feel we had a good home to provide to these kids in need any longer.

Joe even suggested marriage counseling, which I complied for a while, but eventually it fizzled out. This Mr. Nice Guy pattern continued until Joe finally had enough of my lukewarm attempt to stay away from Danny. In hindsight, I know Jess was the reason I kept hanging on. I just couldn't imagine life without her. But regardless, enough was enough. I was being selfish, and I hurt the people closest to me, my husband and my boys. I knew it was time to change my ways once and for all.

2008

Joe asked me to move out of the house, so I moved in with Carrie and her husband Danny for about six weeks. That's when I knew it was time to wake up and smell the coffee. I was at the brink of losing my family, and I couldn't let that happen. I started going to Christian counseling and did everything I could to get things back in good graces with Joe. He could see there was progress but so much damage had been done and trust had been broken.

When Joe agreed to let me come home, I was so happy and excited. It just happened to fall on Valentine's Day, but it was not a good homecoming. I made him his favorite meal of chicken parmesan and had a candlelit dinner waiting for him. His heart just wasn't in it.

When I had my head in the marriage, he didn't, and then when he did, I didn't. Now I was back in the game only to find Joe sitting on the sidelines. We just couldn't seem to find common ground. We spent a lot of time being angry with each other. And that went on for a long time.

In April, Joe lost his job. He got laid off after twenty-one years with the Lee Apparel Co., presently known as VF Jeans Wear. He immediately started his own business called Joe's Home Repair Service. He did everything from electrical to plumbing to painting, carpentry, tile, vinyl, you name it. He could gut a kitchen or a bathroom and rebuild it. He's very talented that way, and he spent the next six years providing for his family with this business.

I got on with the post office as an RCA (rural carrier associate). Basically, that's a glorified term for a substitute mail carrier. I was so proud when I first got that job. I was living the American dream working for the United States Postal Service! It was pretty decent money too.

It was also the same year we started attending Eastside Baptist Church. We just needed something a little bit smaller than our previous church, and Eastside was a lot closer. We loved Pastor Fred and got connected with a Sunday school class that was called "Life Together." That's where we met Ron and Virginia Fleckal. Ron led the class, and we met every Sunday with an amazing group of other Christian believers.

Even with all the turmoil that was going on within our home, we still managed to go to church every week. Looking back, I'm not completely sure how we did it. Joe and I were so angry with each other that I'm not sure if we even liked each other at times.

It was at this pivotal point in my life I was really trying to seek the Lord. I knew I made a critical mistake in my marriage, and I truly wanted to make it right. I had a lot of work to do. I knew God immediately forgave me, but sometimes, it can be hard to forgive yourself. I found that to be true, but I also wanted to live a life pleasing to the Lord.

I was still in the throes of a very serious eating disorder. Joe became aware of it at the time but he never tried to ensure I was getting proper help for it, so it got swept under the rug like everything else, and life plugged along as usual.

2009

I want to share with you a letter that I composed and mailed to my mom, Carrie, and Jessi. It reflects where I was emotionally and spiritually at the time.

I had a revelation and just wanted to share it with those closest to me...my wonderful mother and two beautiful sisters. You know the worst in me and still love me unconditionally and have always been there for me any time night or day. Thank You for that. I love you so very much. God has really been working through me. Now, I may be a slow learner but when I allow myself to listen and be obedient, I hear Great things from my Heavenly Father.

Over the past 10 months I've been singing the same tune...The Blue's. It goes something like this, "My husband has been distant. He hasn't been very nice. He's been hateful and rude at times to me and the boys. He shows no emotion. He's disrespectful. I'm in a cold and lonely marriage". I've had talk after talk about what I physically and emotionally need and he seems so far away most of the time. In turn, I have also hardened my heart against him for the way I have felt mistreated. This goes back a very long time in our relationship. We just never really seem to be on the same page. If you ever think things are bad, try throwing adultery in the mix...not recommended. So, I've been praying for God to soften Joe's heart and show him Love and Compassion. But what about my little ole heart? The 1st thing God has shown me is I need a heart transplant every bit as much as my husband.

Now, Joe and I have had many "talks" over the last few months. They all consist of me crying out to him with all my needs and wants. Well, it was revealed to me the other day during another one of our "talks" that Joe hasn't forgiven me. Big surprise. I knew he hadn't. When you can't forgive somebody, no matter who or what it is, even your spouse, you harbor resentment and bitterness. It's extremely hard when you're living under the same roof with that person. He's completely shut me out and basically checked out of our marriage. That explains his behavior. As you know, I spent 2007 in a world of my own. All I cared about was Heather. I hurt the people closest to me without batting an eye...oblivious to my destructive behavior. Joe spent that same year trying to mend the past and make-up for pushing me into the arms of another. He did all he knew how to do to win me back. His efforts failed and the wall was built. It crushed him and he told himself he was done trying. The 2nd thing God has shown me is I can't just check out of my marriage and then check back in whenever I want without any consequences. I can't just say, "OK, I'm better now, let's get back to where we were". I need to fully understand the magnitude in which I hurt Joe. I need to get on my knees everyday before God and ask Him to soften my heart and show Joe the Love and Compassion that my Heavenly Father shows me. The Holy Spirit's not through working in me yet so until I'm delivered, how can I expect Joe to be?

I've been so bitter toward Joe that I actually thought getting the job at the Post Office was ultimately going to be the way I can "escape" my marriage. Right now, as it is, we can't afford to separate or get a divorce and I surely can't support myself so I have felt like I was "stuck" for lack of a better word. Carrie made a good point. She told me it may be God's purpose that we can't afford to separate because he isn't finished with us yet. There's a lot more work to be done. The 3rd thing God has shown me is this job is not meant as an escape but meant to create more income for our Family so I can contribute financially and relieve Joe of some of that burden. When he lost his job, it added so much stress on top of everything else. I understand now the job is meant to help us, not separate us.

I hope this is all making sense to you because it's huge for me to finally hear what I know is coming straight from God. It may sound so simple but I know we are meant to go through things in life so that we can come out stronger, better people. I truly love my husband. I would like to apologize on Joe's behalf because I think in confiding in you about some of the things we've been going through, I may have actually given you a reason to feel some resentment of your own towards Joe. Not intentionally of course. I now see the error of my ways. I simply felt like I was the victim when quiet possibly he was just as much the victim, so to speak. Joe and I could point fingers and place blame but it's really nobody's fault. We've both made our share of mistakes. Now we just need to pull ourselves out of this pit and stand on solid ground.

I told Joe that I wasn't going to give up on him. I told him I understand his feelings and that I know he needs more time. I told him I would let him have his space but my constant prayer is God will soften his heart and mine. I reminded him that with God, all things are possible. I have no doubt, in time, Joe and I will both be better for each other through this. I know I will be.

I felt the need to express what was going on within me. Thanks again for always being there for me. I'm truly Blessed to have you in my life.

I was on a mission to submit to God and prayed every day for restoration in my marriage, to find contentment and to accept Joe for the unique person God created him to be. I wanted it so badly. And I prayed that Joe would love me the way I loved him, unconditionally and with no abandon.

One of the symptoms of NPD is they expect to be recognized as superior, and they have an exaggerated sense of self-importance. What this translates to in the outside world (church, family, friends, scouts) is Joe wanted to be viewed with a perfect life, perfect job, and perfect family. We were normal on the outside looking in. I actually enjoyed family events and church and scout gatherings, because that's when I got the best of Joe. He was always "happy go lucky" with a smile on his face. Everybody liked Joe.

Ironically, that's what Koen disliked the most. He could see Joe one way in public and another at home. It was an emotional rollercoaster. I tried to keep things on an even keel at home, because I didn't want my kids to suffer, but it was hard.

Koen was always involved in theater and later was cast in a few productions in high school. He played the violin all through middle school and high school.

Isaiah was involved in Cub Scouts and Boy Scouts. Every Monday was Scout night. Joe was very involved and would go on monthly campouts throughout Isaiah's scouting years. I was part of the Mother's Club and served as secretary, which was a way for scout moms to get involved. He would eventually move up the ranks to Scouting's highest honor, Eagle Scout.

Joseph ended up going into real estate and made a pretty good career out of that.

In 2005, Jerimie had a daughter, Kevanah. A couple years later, he ended up relocating to Texas when his mom moved there. That's where he would eventually meet his wife, Amanda, and they would end up with full custody of Kevanah.

I would go over to Gram and Grandpa's every week to mow their grass. Grandpa ended up losing almost all his vision, which required him to give up driving and his carpentry. The least I could do was maintain their yard, and it gave me a good excuse to visit on a regular basis. I cherish those precious memories with them.

And through all this we were still able to maintain a relationship with our little Princess Jess. Danny met Brandi, and they were married a few years later. They would allow us to get Jess several times a year. We never missed holidays or birthdays where she was concerned. I would always contact Brandi to make arrangements, and I never went over there without Joe. I wanted him to know he could trust me, and that part of my life was in the past.

2010

With Joe being in full swing of his home repair business, he would sometimes get repeat clients. This one particular female client he got a bit too close to. She wasn't married, but she lived with a guy, so she was definitely in a relationship. I caught wind of their friendship and confronted both of them. I just randomly showed up at her house, in which they had just returned from lunch together, and told them how inappropriate their friendship was. She didn't like that and told me I wasn't welcome there anymore. That confirmed to me that she didn't want me to come between them. He claimed it was nothing and said that what he was doing didn't come close to what I had done to him. I told him how it wasn't right getting so close to someone of the opposite sex. He got really mad when I started checking his phone. I never felt the need before, but I couldn't trust him.

I thought maybe we needed some space, so I eventually moved in with my brother that summer. BoBo never married or had children, so it worked out. I was still working at the USPS, but because I was a sub and was only guaranteed Saturdays, I also worked at Club 7 Fitness. I knew it was a temporary separation, but couldn't have afforded a place of my own anyway.

Things seemed to get better, so I moved back home with Joe and the boys. But it didn't last long. In October that year, our granddaughter Karlie was born. I remember intercepting a text saying, "Congratulations Grandpa! I love you." WHAT? HOW?

So, I ended up back at BoBo's. He's an electrician and works for the union, and sometimes he would have to go out of state for work. I watched the house and his dogs while he was away. I was there over Thanksgiving and Isaiah's birthday that year. I even put a Christmas tree up during my stay in December.

Joe and I started going back to marriage counseling with the same counselor as the first time. I remember him telling Joe that because he's in business for himself, he has the ability to choose his clients and encouraged him to discontinue any future work for this woman. Eventually, she went away, and I moved back home, and I never heard from her again.

2012

If you can't see a pattern by now, my relationship with Joe has always been an uphill battle. No matter what, he was my husband, and I never gave up on him. Never stopped loving him.

This is the year I started selecting a "Word of the Year." I got the idea from an autobiography written by Author Debbie MaComber titled *Knit Together*. You choose a word that has meaning for you personally and reflect on it all year long. I would always write my word on an index card and include a definition and one to two scripture verses.

My word for 2012 was Faithful. 2 Corinthians 5:7 says, "We live by Faith, not by sight." (In the last pages of this story you'll find all my words from 2012 to the present.) I was bound and determined to be faithful to the Lord, my marriage, my relationships, my work, my diet, and my exercise. It was the beginning of a tradition I wouldn't think of ever giving up now that I've done it for so many years. If this is a new concept to you, I highly encourage you to give it a try. You won't regret it, I promise.

I'm going to share a letter that I wrote to Joe in February of this year. I debated if I should include it or not but decided to go ahead with it, so you can see just how strong Satan's grip was and is. He wanted my marriage in a bad way and was not going to give up.

I used to ask God why my marriage couldn't be better. I knew God didn't like divorce, so I always wondered why my prayer was never answered, but then it occurred to me that God gives us free will and with that we make our own decisions. Just because I wanted it and prayed about it didn't mean Joe wanted it. I truly believe Satan used Joe as a vessel for spiritual warfare, and it was happening under my roof! Don't ever underestimate the enemy.

> *Joe, I guess I'm writing because there are some things on my mind and it just seems better to put them on paper. I wish I could talk to you but it's always the same issues that I want to talk about and I usually get the same 'grunt' and 'eye-roll' from you. It's not very welcoming so here we go with a letter.*
>
> *I pray everyday for you, us, the kids, our finances, etc. and I always ask the Lord that I may find contentment in Him and all he's provided for me. Most of the time I'm very content and feel so blessed at where I am in life but there are some days I ask, 'what about me'? I ask that question on a very intimate, personal level...why does it seem that my needs go unmet so much of the time? It's like the things that are really important to me are not important to you. (I feel silly writing...I feel like even through my words on paper you're actually rolling your eyes saying 'here we go again')!*
>
> *It's like, as long as Joe can go on being Joe, and I have no expectations, things are great with you. You don't have to tell me you love me, you don't have to wear your wedding band, you don't have to kiss me, you don't have to have sex with me or be intimate in any way. Why? Because Joe doesn't want to. With-holding all that from me is just selfish. God intended for those things to be shared between spouses. I feel like my feelings are just swept under the rug and forgotten. My needs are unmet in so many ways. Why am I telling you this? Because this is one of those times my 'love tank' is EMPTY!*

Don't get me wrong Joe! I know you must love me in your own way. You work hard, you come home every night, you provide for this family and take care of us. That's great! I notice those things and I'm not belittling that. Those are the things that I find security and contentment in. But that's not what this letter is about. It's about me and my feelings. They do matter and they are important. I just thought you should know.

Always & Forever, Heather

This has always been our pattern. I felt unloved in the marriage, tried to talk about it, things seemed okay for a while, and then back to a cold shoulder.

I didn't know it at the time, but that was Joe's way of always staying in control. He wasn't going to do anything until he was ready, everything was on his terms. Little things, to me, like wearing his wedding ring. I wanted him to wear it and never could understand that if it was so important to me why he couldn't just put it on. And now I know it's because with NPD their selfishness (usually extreme) is at the expense of others, plus the inability to consider others' feelings at all. He didn't care about my feelings, and he refused to give up control.

By now, Koen was living in Columbia, Missouri, attending Mizzou. He couldn't wait to get out of the house and on his own. He has always been very independent anyway. He was living in an apartment with a roommate, attending classes and working as a server at Chili's, away from home, just the way he liked it. I felt bad that my son felt that way about home, but I didn't take it personally. Koen and I have always had a very close relationship, and we continue to do so to this day.

Joe and I had been looking for some property with the help of Joseph. It sure is nice to have a realtor in the family. Joe wanted something with some acreage, and in April, we found the perfect house, or so we thought.

It was a lovely ranch style home that sat on three acres with a big, beautiful red barn in Peculiar, Missouri. I didn't really want to live in Peculiar, because it was about a forty-five-minute drive to Independence where we went to church and Scouts, and most of Joe's clients were in the city. But we really liked the house (and the barn).

The house needed a ton of work, but we got it for a good price, and I literally just got hired at the QuikTrip Distribution Center in Belton. I had to get out of bed at 3:00 A.M. to be at work at 4:30 A.M. I was usually off work around noon and would meet Joe and Isaiah at the Peculiar house with lunch (and free donuts), and we would put in several hours of work there.

Joe bought new windows for the house. It got a new roof, we pulled out old carpet for new carpet, had the hard wood floors finished, patched walls, built walls and painted walls, and Joe rehabbed the bathrooms. It really was a labor of love. We moved in on July 14th.

Two days after we moved in, on July 16th, I was unpacking a box when I got a phone call that my mom and Robert had been in a serious car crash. I immediately dropped what I was doing and went to Centerpoint Hospital in Independence, Missouri.

Mom and Robert were in the emergency room and both had serious injuries. It was so scary seeing them in this condition, bloody and in so much pain. My mom had been behind the wheel and another driver cut them off, so she had to gun it to get out of the way. When she did, she swerved a hard left, flew over a ditch and into a church yard, slamming into their brick sign.

The scripture on the sign was Psalm 34:3, "Glorify the Lord with me; let us exalt his name together." It was a miracle they lived that day, and I praise God for sparing their lives. The words that were left visible on the sign were "The Lord with me, exalt His name together." The Lord was definitely with them and may we always exalt His name!

My mom lost a lot of blood, because she had a head laceration that ruptured a vein. She was left with fourteen staples in her scalp and received a blood transfusion of four pints. She also fractured her left tibia (shin bone) and fibula (calf bone), leaving her ankle joint crushed as well as a fractured right foot.

Robert had a fractured and crushed left hip socket, a fractured left patella (kneecap), a fractured left wrist and a fractured right tibia. They both had to have multiple surgeries before and after their hospital stay.

They spent three weeks at Centerpoint Hospital and another three weeks at MidAmerica Rehabilitation Hospital. Once they were able to return home, they had to have home health care nurses and physical therapists assisting them. They were both unable to work and were experiencing a real financial hardship.

Carrie, Jessi, Brian, and I all pitched in for our mom and Robert, helping out in different ways from paying bills to running errands, cleaning the house, doing laundry, keeping track of their medication, and keeping up on yard work, just to name a few.

They received their settlement from the accident right before their home went into foreclosure. Fortunately, they were able to pay off their mortgage with that money. Robert ended up going back to work for the Shawnee Mission School District after twelve months. My mom ended up on disability.

While we were going through all this, Joe decided he wanted to move back to Independence. He said he was too far away from clients, so after a short three months, we packed and moved, again. Luckily for us, the market wasn't very good at the time, and our house on Hanthorn was available to move back in to.

Joe was extremely nice to me for a while after that. Don't get me wrong; it's not like Joe didn't have any good times, but he was uncharacteristically pleasant to be around, and I think it's because I was so accommodating to moving back, and he genuinely appreciated it. I was just like "Are you serious? I literally just put the last picture on the wall, and you want to move back!" It was inconvenient, and he knew it, but we did it just the same.

At this point Joe had sold all of his previous rental properties a few years back. We debated on whether we wanted to sell the house or rent it. In the end, we decided to rent it and got lucky with good tenants that rented the house for about eighteen months.

Life plugged along as usual. Isaiah was in middle school, Joe was self-employed, and I was still working at QuikTrip. We continued attending church and Scouts. Things seemed pretty normal.

2014

Carrie teaches second grade at Franklin Smith Elementary School in Blue Springs, Missouri. Ironically enough, it just so happened to be where we attended school when we were kids. That summer she told me that one of their night custodians was going to be leaving, and if I was interested in the job, I should apply, and she would put in a good word for me with her principal, Jan Castle. I'll be honest, I never really thought about that line of work before, but it was a natural fit, because I'm very clean and organized by nature.

I was still working at the QT Distribution Center, but it was a forty-minute drive and the custodial pay was three dollars more per hour. Plus, I was always tired, because I had to get up so early, and I never felt rested. So, on a whim, I applied, not exactly sure what to expect.

Jan Castle and her assistant, Casey Brownsberger, interviewed me on a beautiful summer day right there in her office at FSE. It went so smoothly that I walked out of there feeling extremely confident, not to mention Jan basically told me I had the job. I knew she still had more candidates to interview, so I held off on submitting my resignation at QT until this job was confirmed.

Needless to say, I started my new job as a night custodian at FSE, home of the Mustangs, on August 14th, the first day of the 2014 –

2015 school year. I was super excited and so was Carrie. We were tickled pink to be working together. The only downfall was that Isaiah was a sophomore in high school, and my time with him was very limited.

My hours were 3:30 to midnight, Monday through Friday. Isaiah would get home from school, and I would literally have fifteen minutes with him before I had to leave for work. I made sure I was up at 6:00 A.M. to fix him a little breakfast and see him off to school. The good news was that he was old enough to be home by himself. It was just my lack of time with him that I regretted.

That same year in October, Joe decided to apply for a maintenance position with the Independence School District. He was getting a bit burned out on his home repair business and was looking for a change. It didn't surprise me that they hired him because of his expertise in that area. He got on the evening shift, so we were both working the same schedule. It just seemed meant to be at the time.

For giggles and grins, I would like to set the record straight for those that don't know that there is a difference between a custodian and a janitor. Although most people view them as the same occupation, a janitor is usually employed by a corporation. For instance, a business may hire a janitorial service to clean the bathrooms, empty the trash, vacuum the floors, and dust the cubicles.

A custodian, on the other hand, is responsible for so much more. Not only are we cleaning, but we are also in charge of maintaining the building. In fact, the word custodian comes from the word custody. We have custody of the building, including maintenance and grounds. We cut the grass and make sure the lawn is presentable to the public in the spring and summer months and are in charge of snow removal for the safety of staff and students in the winter. We repair things such as plumbing and electrical needs, as well as painting walls, waxing floors, and replacing air filters.

It's really a lot more than just slinging a mop or pushing a trash can. It's definitely not a very glamorous job, but I found it rewarding. I was known as Miss Heather to the staff and students.

I got my feet wet that first year. Being on nights was very routine, which I enjoyed. For the most part I got to work independently, because everybody goes home at the end of the day leaving the custodians in the evening. Sometimes there were activities that took place at night, such as monthly performances put on by the students in which we would have to set up 350 chairs and take them down (a janitor wouldn't be expected to do that, lol) among other things such as basketball, Girl Scouts, PTA meetings, etc.

2015

That's where I met my friend Bonita. She was on the day shift my first year, and we hit it off. I learned so much from her, especially during summer cleaning. Floors had to be stripped and waxed, and Franklin Smith had tile hallways, so it was a big job. Every room in that building from classrooms to bathrooms got extra special treatment from the light fixtures to the flooring. Paint got freshened up, and everything else got spruced up.

In April 2015, Joe and I bought a sweet little house on Santa Fe from my Aunt Jane and Uncle John, my dad's brother. We were able to acquire it with the sale of the Peculiar house. It needed some home repairs, and the yard needed a lot of attention. We thought it would be a great place to live once Joe retired and Isaiah was out of the house. We talked about adding onto the south side of the house by extending the bedroom, bathroom, and kitchen. We figured it would be a few years down the road.

In the meantime, Koen had graduated from the University of Missouri in December 2014 and was living back at home until he figured out his housing options. Obviously we weren't ready to live in the Santa Fe house yet, so it only seemed like the right thing to do was rent it out to Koen. He got a roommate, Deborah, and that was all she wrote.

It was also convenient to have our son as a tenant, because that would allow us to go over there and take care of the yard work or whatever else needed to be done at our leisure. There were a lot of trees that needed trimming and so much poison ivy to get rid of. Joe was also able to use the garage as needed which was where he stored the riding mower and other tools.

That summer, Jan Castle and Casey Brownsberger got transferred to other schools and were replaced with Mona Dunn as principal and Michael Compton as assistant. It was also the same year that Bonita and I mutually decided she would go on evenings and I would go on days. It was another answer to a prayer for me. It's nearly unheard of to transfer to days, in the same building, after only one year.

I started the 2015 – 2016 school year as the day custodian and couldn't have been happier. Not only was I able to finally be home in the evenings with Isaiah, Carrie and I got to see each other daily. It was a good gig, and I really enjoyed my job. When you work during the day you are basically at the beck and call of staff and students as needed. I would get emergency calls that a student got sick or a bathroom needed attention or someone had a bloody nose, etc.

Then there was lunch duty. It still blows me away just how much food gets wasted and goes in the trash every day. After lunch was over, I would pick up the cafeteria tables and clean the floor and put them back down for the next day. Then I would go into the kitchen and take out trash and mop the floor. A lot of repetition and being able to be flexible was just par for the course.

That same year, Joe got to move from evenings to daytime as well. It was always nice to be on the same schedule. By this time, Isaiah was working on his last few required merit badges to reach his Eagle Scout. So much work went into scouting. It was really an investment of time for all of us. Joe was a leader in the troop and went to every Monday night meeting with Isaiah (with the exception of working nights that one year).

I was a part of the Mother's Club. Our big planning event and only fundraiser was the annual chili supper. It was a lot of work but well worth the effort. The money raised really benefited the troop financially.

Then there were the monthly campouts even in the winter. I remember feeling guilty at times when I was home in my cozy, warm bed, and I thought of the guys out there in tents. Then I realized they were out there by choice, and I didn't feel so bad. It was nice to have a weekend to myself at times, but I was always glad for their return.

In the summer, they would go to Camp Bartle for ten days. That's when the temps were extremely hot. They would have visitors on Sunday, so I had the opportunity to see where they camped and got to take a tour of the grounds to see what they did throughout the week. We would also make a trip into town to get a Peach Nehi float and make a point to stop by the Osceola Cheese Factory on our way home. Such great memories.

2016

At this point, I was still going to Gram and Grandpa's every week. In the summer, I would mow their yard and plant flowers for Gram in a flower bed that Aunt Jane and I built out front. I enjoyed it, and I felt it was the least I could do for these wonderful people that have done so much for me. After I would finish cutting the grass, I would go inside, hot and tired, and Gram would always have a cold drink waiting for me, usually a Diet Coke, and I would sit and visit for a while. Even once mowing season was over, I maintained my weekly visits, mostly on Saturdays. Gram was my friend, my confidant, and I cherished every minute with her. Grandpa too. I never took them for granted.

The latter part of March Grandpa ended up in the hospital with some health issues. He had passed out, and Gram found him on the bathroom floor, so she called Uncle John to come over. Grandpa was taken to Centerpoint Hospital and admitted for dehydration. They ran some tests and got some fluids in him and released him after two days.

The very next day, Gram went to see her doctor, because she had been feeling extremely run down. At first she thought maybe she was just stressed out with everything going on with Grandpa. But after her exam, the doctor sent her to the hospital right away, because she had some fluid around her lungs. She was in the hospital for five nights (six days). They did a procedure and extracted 1.5 liters out of her. Wow, that's a lot. When she came home, Grandpa and Katie, their little Yorkie, were waiting on the front porch for her.

Everyone, including Gram, thought she would bounce back to her normal self, but she never really did. I would go over there and find her still wearing her nightgown, which was totally out of character for her. We're talking about a lady that would put her lipstick on everyday. Grandpa didn't seem to understand that Gram needed her rest, and he kept making demands, because he was used to her waiting on him.

Gram had a follow up visit with her doctor ten days later, and he immediately had her admitted in the hospital again. They had to drain more fluid from around her lungs. It was difficult to see my strong Gram so frail and weak. While she was in the hospital this time, they had to insert a port so that when she got discharged a home health care provider could come by three times a week to drain the fluid.

As all this is happening, Grandpa had been doing some really strange things like putting his pants on backwards and his shoes on the wrong feet. Then he wandered over to the neighbor's house wearing one of Gram's blouses. It broke my heart. Why do people have to get old? It's so sad.

My gram had a great attitude, like she did with everything else in life. She was one of the strongest Christians I had ever known, and she was right with the Lord. She told me he had a plan, and she was in His hands. I couldn't have said it better myself.

A few days later, when she came home, I mowed the grass and mulched and planted flowers. Joe came with me to run the weed eater and remove some leaves and debris. We really spruced up the yard that day.

Grandpa was just getting worse by the day. Gram had to call Aunt Jane to come over there about four times through the night, because he kept getting out of bed, stumbling through the house flipping light switches off and on. By now Gram was in a hospital bed that was set up in the living room and was on oxygen. She couldn't handle Grandpa anymore. He was too much.

They were both declining at a rapid rate. Dad and Uncle John had been looking into assisted living for Grandpa. Aunt Jane, Carrie, and I would take turns spending the night. Grandpa would get out of bed and try to unlock the front door, so he had to start sleeping with a rail on the side of his bed. He started having accidents which required him to wear adult pull-ups.

We would do chores for them while we were there like laundry, taking out the trash, loading the dishwasher, and making the bed. We would make sure they were eating and taking their pills, and we were journaling everything. My gram always had her nails done, and I can remember painting them for the very last time. I also remember the day I lay in bed next to her as we held hands and talked for a while.

She just wasn't getting any better, and Grandpa was being moved to an assisted living home down the street the very next day, which just happened to be my dad's birthday. It was just so sad to watch him leave the house he had built more than sixty years before and to know that they would never be together again.

It was April 30, 2016, and Carrie, Jessi, Brooklyn, Jayden (Jessi's daughters), and I were at Gram's, looking at photo albums, reminiscing, for what would be the last time that we were all together in the house. Gram complained about chest pains, and she never complained, so I knew it was serious. I called Aunt Linda, and she and Uncle Gary came over, and we loaded her in the car and off to the hospital we went, again, for the last time.

The next day all her kids and grandkids were gathered around in the waiting room, and we all took turns visiting Gram around her bedside. Jessi brought in a platter of Subway sandwiches for all of us to have something to eat while we were there. Gram was not doing well and was on a morphine drip that was dispensed every two hours.

The following day, she was moved from Centerpoint Hospital to the same nursing home that Grandpa was in. It was nice that he was able to sit next to her, even though at this point she was under hospice care and unresponsive. Her respiratory system was slowing down, and she was given little sponge swabs in her mouth.

Grandpa seemed to understand when he was told Gram had cancer and is going to Heaven. Jessi talked to Grandpa about accepting Christ in his heart so he could go to Heaven too. That was amazing! Hallelujah!

On Friday, May 6, 2016, five days after arriving at the nursing home, my little gram took her last breath here on Earth. I know Heaven was rejoicing while Gram was greeted with open arms by our Heavenly Father. When you lose somebody so close to you it's a pain and a void so deep but so sweet at the same time, because her body was whole again and no longer in pain. I'm so proud she was my gram, and I can look forward to the day she welcomes me with open arms.

So much happened in such a short period of time. Family members continued to make regular visits to see Grandpa. And we all pulled together to get the house cleaned out and ready to sell. It was a difficult time, but we persevered through it.

A few months later, my mom asked me if I was interested in joining a TOPS Club, and at first, I was skeptical. The reason why is because the only thing I knew about TOPS was that my gram belonged for as long as I could remember, and I associated it as a "fat club for old ladies." Seriously! That may sound funny to you and a bit stereotypical, but that's what Gram called it, her fat club. I didn't want to be in a fat club.

Needless to say, I decided to give it a try, because I thought if nothing else, it's something my mom and I can do together on a weekly basis. So, we visited a chapter in Independence on November 1st and felt like we made an immediate connection and joined that evening with no regrets.

For those of you that don't know, TOPS stands for Take Off Pounds Sensibly. It's an organization that's been around since 1948 and was started by a lady named Esther Manz in Milwaukee, Wisconsin. Those first meetings took place around Esther's kitchen table with two friends who had a desire to support each other to thinner figures and better health.

The premise for this organization is to provide a support system for men and women to take off and keep off pounds sensibly. We emphasize that it's not the number on the scale but how you feel about yourself. We all set our own weight loss goal and have to get a letter from the doctor, because the focus is on health. Once you reach your goal, you then become a KOPS, Keep Off Pounds Sensibly.

Individuals can find a local chapter by going online and choosing a meeting place close to their home according to a day and time that fits your personal schedule. You can visit as many chapters as you want for free until you find the one that's the best fit for you. Once you join, you pay thirty-two dollars (annually) and monthly dues to your chapter that are usually five dollars, depending on the chapter.

I'm putting a good word in for TOPS, but on a more serious note, this club saved my life. I have had an unhealthy relationship with food for years, and I found something that I can belong to with other members that have the same exact issues as me. We all come together to support each other as we are held accountable as we face the scale each and every week.

Each chapter has a leader, co-leader, weight recorder, assistant weight recorder, secretary, and treasurer. I've had the pleasure of holding the position of leader with my mom as my co-leader and find it to be very rewarding.

Each week, as members arrive, they weigh in then once the meeting starts, we say our pledge, do roll call, welcome new members, have a program on a variety of food related/healthy topics, take care of business, all within an hour's time. We give awards to recognize members achievements, participate in Fall Rallies, SRD (State Recognition Days), and community events.

My mom came up with the idea of purchasing matching T-shirts to wear when we attended these events. We decided on coral-colored shirts with black lettering. The front left said, "TOPS MO 0331 Independence." That's our chapter ID. The back spelled out WARRIOR vertically with each letter spelling a word: W—willpower, A—action, R—rededicated, R—resolve, I—intentional, O—organized, R—ready.

It's been a very positive influence in my life. In fact, I reached my KOPS goal in June 2018. It's a struggle from week to week, but for someone that's suffered from an eating disorder, it's a struggle I don't have to do alone. It's much like an AA meeting for an alcoholic. We're all in it together. I'm glad Esther Manz started TOPS, and I'm glad my mom asked me if I wanted to join.

November was a busy month. Isaiah passed his board of review and achieved his Eagle Scout rank. Yay! I was so proud of him. That is a very difficult rank, but I always knew he could do it. We also celebrated Isaiah's eighteenth birthday on the 20th.

I really thought things were going well for Joe and me. The middle of November came another blow to our marriage. He had been texting a coworker. He said it was nothing, but when they're telling each other they enjoy talking to each other with a heart emoji attached, it's a bit much.

On November 30, just six short months after Gram went to Heaven, Grandpa passed away through the night. He had been staying with John and Jane for a couple of weeks, and then he ended up back in the hospital. Poor little guy. He had been in so much turmoil. His mind had really been escaping him. It does my heart good to know him and Gram are together. I miss them both so much.

A couple days before Christmas Eve, on a Saturday, Joe left around 1:45 P.M. and didn't return until 9:00 P.M.. I didn't believe his story about how he answered alarm calls, and then he lost his phone and retraced his steps, blah, blah, blah. It all sounded bogus to me. He couldn't account for over SEVEN hours to satisfy my curiosity as to his whereabouts.

2017

Joe has an uncanny way of making me mad and then knowing exactly what strings to pull to sweet talk me back to "everything's going to be okay." This has been his pattern for as long as I've known him. All the way back to Christmas Eve 1996 when he stood me up.

I've had a gym membership for years and not once has my husband ever shown an interest in personal fitness. All of a sudden, he joined a group from work to get in shape to kick off the new year. Some "Amazing Race" contest employees could participate in. Come to find out, the same woman he was texting in November was part of this group.

My mom's best friend worked at Kohl's department store. Joe was spotted with the other woman shopping for gym shorts and tennis shoes. I didn't find this out until much later, of course, but that is a symptom of NPD. He didn't think about the consequences, exhibited selfish behavior, did what he wanted to, and lied his way out of it later. Typical.

So, my guess at this point is they've been spending time together, talking, getting closer. He's telling her a sob story about how he's in this unhappy marriage, and I'm this terrible wife. Boohoo.

I sound bitter, because I was. I couldn't believe it. After all we've been through he thought it was okay to have a close friend of the opposite sex. Then I intercepted a text message from her asking if she was going to see him that day, which was a Sunday. She was programmed on his phone as "Alarm." I knew he was being sneaky, because he gave her a fictitious name.

I'd had enough. I didn't want to live with someone I couldn't trust. I went as far as putting a deposit down on an apartment for myself and Isaiah, but once I realized there was a one-year lease, I got cold feet. I thought we needed space but that seemed like more time than I wanted to be away from home.

It just so happened that my niece, Courtney (Carrie's daughter), was going through a divorce at the time and could use a roommate. I ultimately decided to move in with Courtney in the latter part of January instead of the apartment. This was meant to be a separation to once again give us clarity of what we want out of this marriage and get our priorities straight.

This was our fourth separation with two attempts at marriage counseling. Every time we separated, I was the one who would move out, and it was always meant to be on a temporary basis. This was no different.

Unfortunately, Joe never seemed to miss me while I was away. The whole time I was at Courtney's, praying for things to improve in our marriage, he didn't take it seriously. It was like a vacation to him. Here's a quote that rings true, "If your absence doesn't affect them, your presence never mattered."

We held an Eagle Scout ceremony and reception for Isaiah in March. After months of planning, handmade centerpieces, refreshments, cake, and punch, it all came together beautifully. There were about eighty people in attendance. It was a great day and well deserved for Isaiah. It was just wonderful to see him shine.

Joe and I also celebrated our nineteenth anniversary in March. He took me to dinner at a Mexican restaurant, and I stayed the night with him. It was a very pleasant time.

In the ten weeks that I lived with my niece, nothing ever changed, there was absolutely no progress made other than the fact that I thought the other woman was out of the picture. I guess I was just blinded by the fact that I missed home and wanted to return to what was familiar to me.

Two weeks before I moved back home, we decided not to see each other or talk or text. This was going to be the moment of truth. I was digging deep, praying for strength and for God to really work through Joe.

Then I get this random text message. It's a photo of Joe's hand wearing his wedding ring. I'm pleasantly surprised and excited. But here's Joe's tactic; he knows if he puts on the ring, he has me, hook, line and sinker. I know you must be thinking how naïve I am, but I was looking for any excuse to get back to my life, so I took the bait. Just a few days later, after I returned home, the ring was off, and he started putting distance between us, again.

So, we're three weeks into June, and Joe had been planning this Route 66 road trip. He was going to be taking the 1966 Cadillac, had maps and brochures, the whole nine yards. I told him I had vacation days I could take and would love to go with him. I mean, isn't that what married couples do? Go places together and spend time together? He basically told me I wouldn't want to go, that he had an agenda, and I would be bored. I have to admit, I thought it was weird, but okay, I gave him my blessing to go take this solo road trip and come back renewed, if that's what he wanted.

The morning he left, I kissed him goodbye and told him to have a fun, safe trip. But the whole time he was gone, I had this nagging feeling and felt uneasy. A full week later he returned, bursting at the seams, full of stories and souvenirs and lots of pictures.

In July, I took an Alaskan cruise with Koen, Isaiah, BoBo, and Kathy. Again, I thought it was weird that Joe backed out of this family vacation, because I figured he would love Alaska. I didn't fight it though, I just thought I would have a better time without him if he felt pressured into going.

We had the time of our life on that trip. It was fabulous. We started out in Seattle, Washington. We got there a day early to do some sightseeing before we boarded the cruise ship.

Our first port was in Juneau, Alaska. That's where we took a sea plane over these huge glaciers to Taku Lodge where we were fed a "fresh salmon" feast. We saw a black bear up in a tree, and after our feast, he had come down from the tree and was licking the drippings off the grill. It was amazing!

Our next port was in Skagway, Alaska. We got to experience a dog mushing excursion. It was very interesting to hear the history about this sport. And we got to see where and how they train the dogs and got to be pulled by a team of "Mushers," a very fun experience.

We then cruised for a few days on our way to Victoria, British Columbia, Canada. There is so much to do on a ship. We went to the theater several nights and saw a magician, comedian, and talent acts. We went to an ice-skating show and an art auction. There was a casino, art gallery, and arcade. They had shopping and dining. The boys and I went to a couple of formal dinners where I feasted on lobster. BoBo and I even got in the hot tub a couple of times. It was just a jam-packed, fun-filled vacation.

Once in British Columbia, the boys and I went on a whale watching excursion and walked the streets of Canada. It was breathtaking, the whole trip. The first thing I did when I got home was develop all my photos and put together a scrapbook.

By now I had been with the Blue Springs School District for three years. I was looking for a change, so when I found out that the day custodian at James Walker Elementary (JWE) was retiring, I immediately made a cold call to the principal, Dr. Kelly Flax. I introduced myself and told him I was interested in the position. I applied, interviewed, and got the job.

I have to admit, it helped that Dr. Flax not only knew Jan Castle on a professional level, but they just happened to be close friends. So close in fact that their families took camping trips together. When Dr. Flax asked Jan about me, she told him to hire me, so he did.

I started at JWE, home of the Warriors on August 1st. I was proud to be a Warrior. Remember our TOPS shirt? Not only was I a Warrior in TOPS, I was now a Warrior at work. The definition of warrior, according to Google, is a brave or experienced soldier or fighter. More specifically, a warrior is someone who follows a code of conduct that determines their very values and ethics.

JWE is where I met my good friend Linda. She was one of the evening custodians at the time. Her and I had a great rapport from the beginning. Linda is officially retiring in December, 2020 which is very well deserved. She will be missed around the workplace, but even more than that, she's a friend for life. She's going to have to do a lot more than retire to escape from me.

I love my job. Don't get me wrong, we all have bad days here and there, and my job requires a lot of things most people wouldn't want to do, but it works for me. Just a couple months later, it was our school's turn to highlight a staff member, and since I was the newbie, Dr. Flax said it was an easy decision to make. He wrote up an article about me that made the front page on our district's newsletter.

> *James Walker Elementary is fortunate to have Heather Pinter as our Day Custodian. When a long time JWE Custodian retires, you have a little anxiety on how to fill the shoes. Little did we know what was coming our way. A JWE teacher captures the essence of Heather Pinter, and her immediate impact on JWE by saying, "Heather stepped in from day one with a smile on her face. Any time I have asked her to do something (big or small) she is right on top of things, again, with a smile on her face. You can tell she takes pride in her job and loves the students and staff at JWE. I appreciate her positive attitude and willingness to always help others."*
>
> *Every day, Heather greets staff and students with a smile. She is quick to offer a helping hand to anyone who needs it. She is a friendly presence and a great addition to the JWE staff.*
>
> *Another staff member notes that "not only does Heather do an amazing job of keeping our school shining, she is a smiling face to welcome our students each morning. Heather is also a key player during our lunch time. She maintains a clean environment all while taking time to get to know the students at JWE. No matter the question or request, Heather does her job with a contagious positive attitude. Heather goes above and beyond each day for the students and staff at JWE."*

As a school, each and every day brings new challenges and opportunities. Heather is an important piece of our day to day operation, and embraces her job with a great attitude. More often than not, Heather sees a need and takes care of it before anyone is aware of it.

It's nice to be recognized for a job well done. My mom was proud too, because she printed the article and framed it for me. I thought that was sweet.

It was approximately this time period that I found out Koen chose a homosexual lifestyle. Well, let's put it this way, I knew about it from a couple of years prior, but this was the first time I actually met someone he was dating.

I love my son unconditionally. There's nothing that could ever change that. If we're being completely candid here though, it broke my heart. As a parent, we all have hopes and dreams for our children. From the day Koen was born, I prayed for his future. I wanted him to have a career and a wife and children of his own. I've had to process this as a mom and deal with this in my own way. I wept for the choices that were made and for the grandchildren my first-born son would never give me.

Koen knows my stance on this subject. I firmly believe we were knit together in the womb, and God doesn't make mistakes. Living a gay lifestyle is so acceptable in this modern world that we live in but no matter how you look at it, it's a sin. Nobody's born gay. It's a choice that was made and one that's between Koen and God. It's not my place to judge, and I will accept Koen and love him regardless of his sexuality. 3 John 1:4, "I have no greater joy than to hear that my children walk in the truth." I will never give up that hope.

Jerimie and Amanda had been wanting to move from Texas to Missouri for a while. Joe and I wanted them here as well. It would give us more opportunity to see them and the kids on a regular basis. Kevanah was twelve; Karlie was seven; and Noah was eight months old.

They decided the best way to make the move was for Jerimie to come ahead to Missouri and find a job and a place to get settled while Amanda and the kids stayed in Texas, so we offered him a place to stay while he got on his feet. He ended up getting a job with FedEx in October and found a little house to rent in November.

Amanda and the kids were able to join him three weeks before Christmas. They all came over on Christmas Eve, and we had lasagna for dinner. It was a really good evening.

The next morning, we celebrated Christmas just like we did every other year. Koen, Isaiah, Joe, and I did our gift exchange following brunch with Joseph and Tim.

It's been a tradition for the last several years that we go to Jessi's home in the evening to celebrate with my mom and Rob and the whole family. Joe used to participate in all our family functions. All of a sudden, he decided he wanted to stay home that year, so I went to my sister's house without him. I wasn't going to put up a fight, and I had a great time, as usual.

By the time I got home, Joe wasn't there, and he couldn't be reached. Go figure. Lately he had been gone for long hours at a time, but I trusted him, nevertheless. He made it home about thirty minutes later, telling me he had to answer an alarm call. We talked about how my evening went and then turned in for the night.

We had Jerimie and Amanda and the kids over for New Year's Eve. Isaiah and his girlfriend, Hera, were downstairs while the rest of us were hanging out, playing with the kids, eating snacks, and waiting for midnight. It was 11:45 P.M., and we had turned on the TV while we were waiting for the countdown.

Joe and I were sitting next to each other on the couch, and I just happened to look at Facebook, and the first post that popped up on my phone had a photo of my husband that I did not recognize. He was opening a gift with a smile on his face. I was surprised to say the least. I showed it to Joe and asked him when and where this was taken and who the other people were in the picture. He lied to me. I don't remember what he said, but it was a lie, because I had to ask him, "Was this picture taken on Christmas night?" You can only imagine the fury when he said yes.

My world turned upside down in an instant. When the realization that he was with another woman's family instead of mine on Christmas, and that she had the nerve to tag him in a post finally hit me; I felt like I had been pushed off a cliff and was reeling through midair, unable to breathe. It took me a minute for this to register. I can remember thinking "Is he leading a double life?" How could this be happening? That was my "Happy New Year 2018."

Photo Gallery

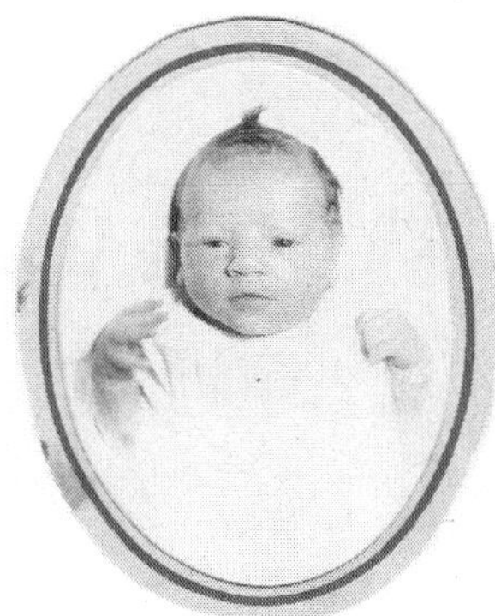

March 15, 1971. My birth photo.

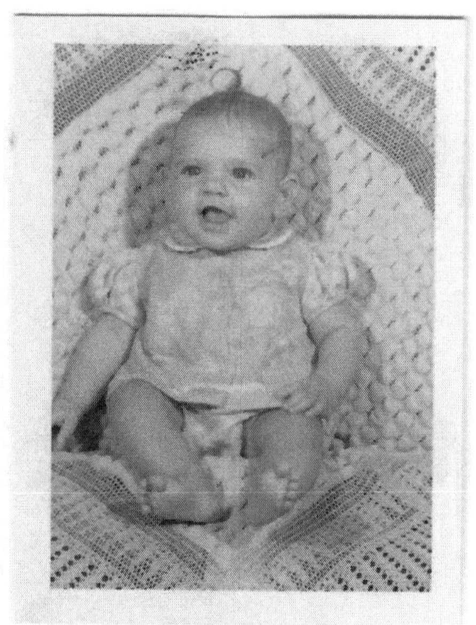

August 5, 1971. Me, at 4 months, 3 weeks.

1973. Me, at 2 years old.

Fall 1968. My mom, Mary Ann Colston, her sophomore year at 16 years old.

July 4, 2010. Me and my beautiful mom at Brian's.

September 19, 2010. Robert and Mom on her birthday at our house in Peculiar, MO.

December 2018. At Mom's church. From left, Jessi, Carrie, me, Brian (Mom centered).

1968.
My dad, Jerry Gaughran, in the Army.

Christmas 2007. Me and my dad at his house.

April 2013.
My dad and Kathy at Carrie's.

April 28, 2018. My dad's birthday at his house. From left, me, Brian, Carrie, Jessi (Dad centered).

March 5, 1972.
Me and Grandpa Colston, Harvey Richard.

July 20, 1975.
From left, Carrie, me, Grandma Colston, Mary Lou.

October 1973. Me camping. Even at a young age I could be found with a cleaning towel in my hand.

Spring 1978.
Me riding my mini-bike, at 8 years old.

Summer 1978. Me and my dad at church reunion the day I got baptized, at 8 years old.

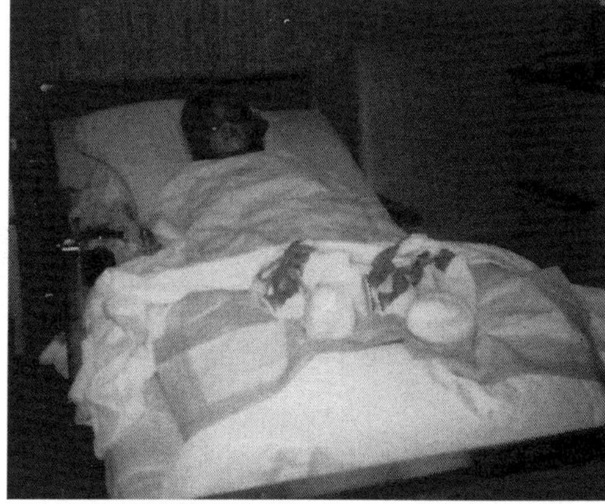

1983.
Me in the hospital after my foot operation, at 12 years old.

Approximately 1950.
My Gram and Grandpa Gaughran,
Ellen (Gouldsmith) and Vince.

April 2008.
Me and Grandpa at my dad's.

July 4, 2013.
Me and Gram at Brian's.

Christmas Eve 1980.
Me playing Mary as we reenacted Jesus' birth. From left, me, Carrie, Brian, Jessi.

Halloween 1977.
From left, Carrie, Brian, Jessi, me.

October 2015.
Our annual Oktoberfest at my dad's. From left, Carrie, Brian, Jessi, me.

Christmas 2019.
From left, Heather, Carrie, Jessi, Brian (our birth order) at Jessi's house.

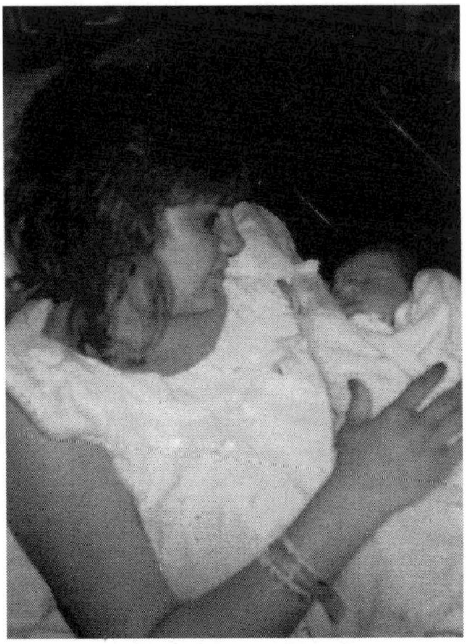

June 22, 1990.
Koen's birth. I was 19 years old.

May 2007.
Koen and me at Silver Dollar City in Branson, MO.

December 20, 2014.
Koen's college graduation at Mizzou, the University of Missouri. He has a degree in Bachelor of Science: Parks, Recreation, and Tourism, with an emphasis in Leisure Management and a Minor in Sociology.

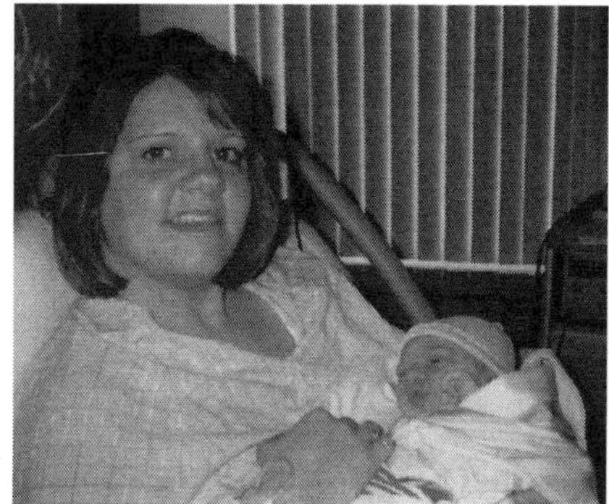

November 20, 1998.
Isaiah's birth. I was 27 years old.

March 4, 2017.
Isaiah's Eagle Scout ceremony.

September 2018.
Isaiah and me at Brian's for our annual birthday bonfire to celebrate Mom and Robert.

Christmas 2000.
Me with Isaiah and Koen
at our annual
Gouldsmith Christmas Party.

Mother's Day 2016.
Me with Isaiah and Koen
at our house on Hanthorn.

March 2017. Disney on Ice: Follow Your Heart. Isaiah and Koen.

August 26, 2005.
Jess in the NICU; the day we brought her home from the hospital; my first time holding her at 6 weeks.

2010. My Princess Jess at age 5.

2016.
At Worlds of Fun when Koen was supervisor.
From left, Isaiah, Jess, Koen.

2016.
Me and Jess at one of her karate competitions.
"Look at all those trophies."

March 7, 1998.
Me and Joe on our wedding day.

December 1999.
Family Christmas photo.
From back clockwise:
Jerimie, Joseph, Koen, me, Isaiah, Joe.

July 4, 2010.
Me and Joe at Brian's.

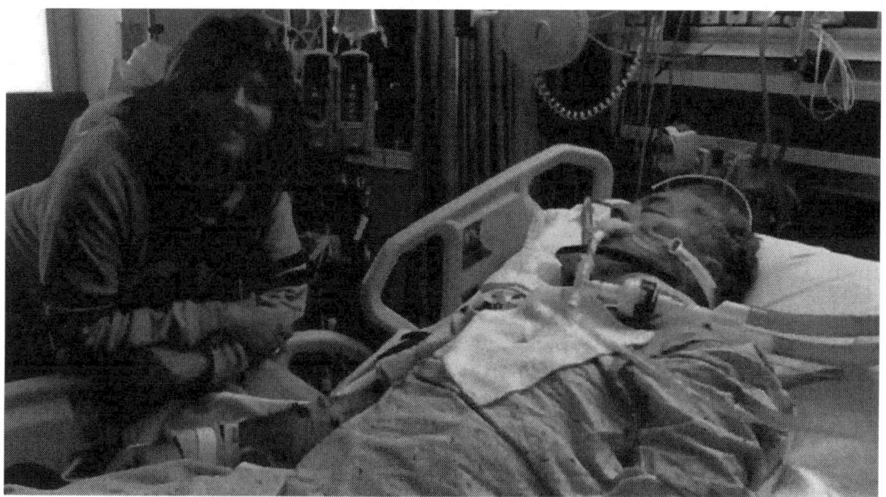

July 26, 2018. The day after Joe's accident.

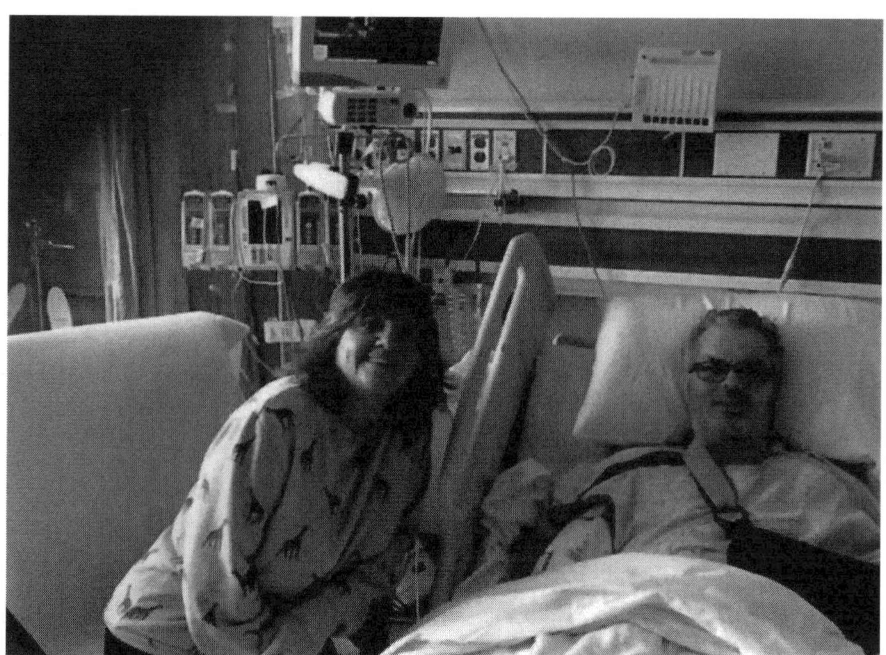

July 28, 2018. The day after Joe was taken off the ventilator.

May 30, 2016. Me feeding my favorite animal at Cheyenne Mountain Zoo in Colorado.

July 16, 2017. Waterfall Trail in Juneau, Alaska. From left, Brian, Koen, Isaiah, me, Kathy.

Septermber 2019. Annual birthday bonfire at Brian's. My nieces, nephews and boys, in birth order: Courtney, Koen, Cole, Nate, Isaiah, Brooklyn, Jayden, Gabe.

October 2019. My TOPS Club preparing to ride in the Halloween parade. From left, Mom, me, Susan, Aunt Deanie.

Halloween 2019. Me with my grandkids. From left, Karlie, Noah, me, Kevanah.

December 2017.
My cat, Jasper.

March 7, 2020.
Me with the buffalo at Lake Jacomo on what would have been our 22nd anniversary.

Warrior photo.
As mentioned in the book, I'm a JWE Warrior, TOPS Warrior and Kingdom Warrior!

2018

Somehow, in the next few minutes, we rang in the New Year and quickly ushered Jerimie and his family out the door. By this time, she had a name (she knows who she is). I knew there had to be more to the story, so I pulled her Facebook page up on the desktop computer and just about flipped my lid. In this woman's cover picture, she was posing next to the 1966 Cadillac on a bridge with a Route 66 sign in view. It was at that very moment that I realized he had taken her with him on his "solo" road trip in July. No wonder he talked me out of going.

I asked him if he'd been having sex with her in which he couldn't deny. How could he do this to me after everything we've been through together? It had been ten years since my bout with infidelity. Did he not remember the pain and suffering and the damage it caused? At that moment I did not know the man I was married to, because that man would NEVER betray me like that.

This is the same woman that I had intercepted text messages a year prior. The one he was in a fitness group with. The one he was at Kohl's with. The one that we separated over. Is she also the reason he didn't want to go with me to Alaska? And what about 2017, when I finally thought things were the best they've ever been between us? No doubt it was because he was living on a permanent high for getting away with his indiscretions.

Unless you've personally gone through this kind of betrayal, it's really hard to describe. I've suffered a lot, and I've tolerated a lot in my marriage, but I never in a million years could have dreamed that Joe would have the capability to pull this off. He did a really good job of lying and cheating. This had been going on right under my nose, and I had no clue.

We didn't go to bed that night. I was hurt and angry. I wanted answers. When and where and how often and why? How could he deny me of the most intimate part of a marriage relationship and so freely give it to another woman? How could he take her on a road trip, sightseeing, visiting little mom and pop restaurants and staying in and out of motels all along the way?

I knew I didn't deserve this. All he could do was tell me she didn't mean anything and how much he loved me and how sorry he was. More like, sorry he got caught. He said he knew he screwed up and didn't want to lose me.

In hindsight, I could have saved myself a lot of heartache down the road if I would have insisted he leave that first night. I should have told him if you want her, you can have her.

The following day I sat next to him when he called her to break it off. I could hear her tell MY husband "You told me you love me on Christmas" and "I thought we were in a committed relationship." Oh boy! This was way more serious than I thought. I knew it was not going to end overnight, especially if he led her to believe he loved her and they were committed to each other. No wonder she felt so confident in posting a photo of him on social media.

I know now what I couldn't have possibly known then, and that's that Joe suffers from a personality disorder that is so distorted that not only was he lying to me to get what he wants, he was lying to her. He never loved her. He used her to fulfill a selfish desire. She was just as much a victim as I was, but she's a big girl, and it was her choice to tangle with a married man.

Satan was pulling the strings here. He knows how to disguise himself and work through people and his mission is to steal, kill, and destroy (John 10:10). My marriage has been on attack for years. I hate to admit it, but I didn't realize that either. I just thought Joe had made a mistake, and if he really was sorry, we could fix it. But I knew it would take some time after personal experience, so I told Koen he was going to have to move out of the Santa Fe house so his dad could move in. I made it easy for Joe. I realize that now.

This was Joe's mistake, and I wasn't going to leave my house this time around. It was a hardship for Koen and his roommate to have to move on such short notice. Koen ended up staying with me for a couple of weeks until he made some arrangements with friends. He knows he could have stayed longer, but honestly, he didn't want to. He didn't want to be in the middle of this storm that was brewing, and I couldn't blame him.

It was hard enough on Isaiah. He was so angry with his dad. I think he was hurt more than anything. It affected him. It affected all of us.

Joe moved into the Santa Fe house on Martin Luther King Jr. Day. It was still our house, and the idea was for him to clear his head and get his priorities straight. He told me he loved me and wanted to work things out. Joe assured me he didn't want our marriage to end in divorce, and I desperately wanted to believe him, so I gave him a chance.

He immediately started doing some home repairs, such as replacing the kitchen faucet and patching and painting the walls. Anything to keep busy.

The early part of February, he couldn't be reached, so I drove over there, and to my dismay, there was a little black car in the driveway. I let myself in with my house key, and there she sits on the couch. It was the first time I met her face to face, and I must say, I wasn't impressed. I managed to give them a piece of my mind while keeping my cool. I told them I wasn't interested in this love triangle and that he has been lying to both of us. Then I left.

He tried to call me that night, but I wouldn't answer the phone. He sent me a text message telling me she was gone. A few days later, it was Valentine's Day. When I got home from work, I had roses, a card, and an apology written in black sharpie on a heart-shaped box of chocolates. A little bit of sweet talk, that's all it took, and he was back in good graces.

The first part of March, I couldn't get a hold of him again, so I showed up over there unannounced. He was home alone, so I stuck around for a bit. He got a text message, so I checked his phone. I had never before taken the time to look at his phone, but under the circumstances, I didn't trust him. It was her, go figure. She had actually invited him to attend a program at her granddaughter's elementary school, which he accepted. When I showed up unexpectedly, he ended up standing her up. Once again, I got mad and left and didn't talk to him for a week. March 7th was our anniversary, so more sweet talk.

Things would appear good for a while and then, boom, he would all of a sudden be unavailable. I always knew when I couldn't reach him, she was involved.

I showed up at his house in mid-April and waited for two hours. I finally called Isaiah and asked him to find her address. Within five minutes, he called with an address and came to pick me up. My biggest regret is getting my nineteen-year-old son involved.

We drove to her house and there sat Joe's truck in her driveway. When they finally opened the front door, I became enraged at the sight of my husband standing next to this woman. When I crossed the threshold and she told me not to come in, I lost my temper. I wasn't so calm, cool, and collected this time. I was so sick and tired of these two lying and cheating that I punched her in the face, and we scuffled a bit. Joe tried to pull me off of her, and I managed to backhand him in the jaw. Not my finest moment.

We stood there arguing, so when the police showed up, we weren't at all surprised. Isaiah was holding a baseball bat which made matters worse. Of course, she pressed charges on both of us, so Joe got to watch his wife and son get handcuffed and hauled off to jail. I remember sitting in the back of the squad car thinking this must be what it's going to take to finally file for divorce.

My son and I both spent our first (and last) night in jail together in cells right next to each other. It was the worst night we have ever experienced. I had a thin mat on the floor and a commode with a roll of toilet paper, but that was it. It was cold and miserable, and it definitely gave me time to think and put things into perspective.

Fifteen hours later, we were released on bond. Hera and Zach, Isaiah's best friend, bailed Isaiah out. Joe bailed me out and drove me back to his house, because that's where I left my car. I told him I thought it was best if we parted ways. He just kept making the same mistake, and I told him "at first it's a mistake, then it's a decision."

I had put my job in jeopardy, because I didn't show up, which is totally out of character for me. That caused our school secretary to reach out to my sister, because she knew Carrie taught at FSE. That got my family involved. I was done. I couldn't believe it had gone this far. I called Joseph that weekend and talked to him about what I needed to do to put the Hanthorn house on the market. For me to be so angry that I threw all rational out the window was not working for me anymore. I should never be forced to get that mad.

My mom's pastor agreed to visit with me. We had a pleasant conversation, and he asked if Joe would be willing to come in the following week. I was surprised when Joe accepted. We went together and heard some biblical truths. Joe, once again, said he was sorry and didn't want me to file for divorce. He talked me into giving it another go around.

It's actually called "love-bombing" and is a classic behavior with NPD. As soon as I would try to back away, he would try that much harder to keep me in his life. He would say all the right things to make me think he'd changed, but soon enough, he'd show me that he never actually changed at all.

May rolled around and things seemed to be going pretty smooth, so I thought. I just randomly decided to drive by Joe's house before work one morning, and lo and behold, there they sat on his front porch drinking coffee. I got out of the car and approached them. He told me he tripped and fell down the stairs the night before and he ended up calling her instead of me. Who does that?

What is wrong with this picture? She's there in the morning which tells me she was there all night. I couldn't believe he would have her in my house, let alone in my bed. I was at such a low point. I had been knocked down emotionally so many times, and I would pick myself back up only to be knocked down again. I didn't want the pain; I wanted the love, but the love came with the pain. I knew I was in a sick, vicious cycle, but I did not know how to break free from it. Joe knew exactly what to say and do to keep me coming back. More love-bombing.

He must have really been pulling one over on her too! It was Memorial weekend, and I was at his house for the night and about 1:45 A.M. I woke up to the most disgusting text messages from her. Apparently she drove by, saw me there, and went on a jealous rage. She basically told me I was a nasty skank, when, where, and how many times they had sex, and that she's been coming over on Tuesdays when I was at my TOPS meeting and that I was a fat ass.

It was extremely inappropriate. I couldn't believe Joe would approve of her talking to me like that. One of the things people with NPD are known for is pitting people against each other. This was a classic case of that. So, of course, we stayed up all night, and he's telling me how crazy she was.

We had a trip already planned the first weekend in June to take the Mercury to Rolla, Missouri for their Route 66 Summerfest and classic car show. We decided to keep our plans, and even though we had a rocky start, we ended up having a really good time.

The funny thing is that every time I had a gut feeling I followed my intuition. And I would ask God to reveal anything to me that needed revealed. The Friday after we returned from our weekend getaway, I had a hunch something wasn't right. I called my cousin, Susan, and we did some driving around. Joe had parked his motorcycle behind her house. The only way you could see his bike was by driving around the street behind her and looking between the houses.

He sure thought he was clever. We sat across the street and waited for him to leave. I sat there and watched my husband pull out onto the street, so we followed him to his driveway. I confronted him, and he shrugged it off saying it was nothing.

My emotions were running high. I was so emotionally broken. I couldn't believe he would go to her again. I contacted an attorney and started the process of filling out divorce papers. I'd seen Joe a handful of times, because Kevanah had volleyball games and Karlie had soccer games. We made it through the 4th of July and seemed to be on good terms. I had checked his phone and didn't find any trace of her. Knock on wood.

It was mid-July, and we had Jess for the weekend. It was this visit that she found out we were separated. She's thirteen by now and seemed to handle the news well. We had taken her to the drive-in on Saturday, and Joe went with me to take her home on Sunday.

Things had been good for the past few weeks, even with talk of divorce, but for some reason, I could sense a distance between us. If you don't know by now, that's a pattern with Joe. When things were going well, he has to sabotage it. When I confronted him about his cool distance between us, he got mad and it started a fight. We parted ways, and I went to work on Monday, as usual.

By Tuesday he was still holding a grudge, so I stopped by after TOPS to try to work things out. He had actually taken his wedding band off, again. I guess when you have an argument with your spouse, it's normal to remove the ring. Anyway, by the time I left, he seemed to be in better spirits.

On Wednesday morning, July 25th, I was at work changing filters on the roof. It was 10:00 A.M., and I received a call from Joseph. He said his dad had an accident and was being taken to Centerpoint Hospital. I left work immediately. By the time I got there, I met with some of his coworkers in the waiting room. I found out he fell fifteen feet from a ladder and hit concrete. It knocked him unconscious, and when he came to, he was disoriented and combative. I guess he gave the paramedics a run for their money.

Joe had to go into emergency surgery to have his spleen removed. He had a head injury, so they did a CAT scan and found that the blood in his head was not expanding. He had to be sedated and put on a ventilator to keep him comfortable. He broke his clavicle and his nose and fractured his orbitals (the facial bones around his eye sockets) which would heal on their own.

When I was given Joe's belongings, I had possession of his cell phone. When I pushed the home button I saw one simple word, "hi," from the person he said he wasn't talking to anymore. The time stamp was just minutes before paramedics were called. There's no way she would have had time to hear about his accident which means she was just randomly reaching out to him that morning without ever knowing that the text would be intercepted. I had divorce papers filled out and ready to file if I saw another line of communication between them, and now my husband was lying in a hospital bed in ICU.

I immediately asked the Lord what I was supposed to do. Joe was clearly going behind my back, keeping in contact with her, and doing a good job of covering his tracks. I had all these questions swirling around in my head.

On top of that, I was dealing with Joe's doctors, his case manager, workman's comp and his superiors with the Independence School District. I did the only thing I thought any wife should do under the circumstances and that was stand by my husband. He was in bad shape, and I couldn't turn my back on him now. Could I?

Joe was in ICU for seven days. Three of those days he was in an induced coma. During that time, I took off work and sat next to him, waiting, praying, and hoping he would survive. My mom spent a lot of time at the hospital, just sitting with me so I wouldn't be alone. I had family and friends that visited and made sure I was eating. I would go home at night to sleep and take a shower, but then I was right there first thing in the morning.

During his hospital stay, Joe had many friends from work come and visit. He also had relatives that came from out of town. His sisters, Theresa and Linda, brother Randy, brother-in-law Gary, and nephew Gabriel came from Colorado. His nephews Randall and Alex came from North Carolina. There was a lot of concern about his outcome. We had a lot of prayer warriors too, just a real outreach of people.

When they first removed the ventilator, Joe was very confused and disoriented, and he didn't comprehend what was going on. He also didn't recognize anybody, including me. Luckily that didn't last long. He had a couple coworkers stop by when the speech therapist fed him applesauce and ice cream for the first time. He was so childlike, watching him begin to recognize people and eat and drink.

Soon after the ventilator was removed, the doctors were very pleased with his progress. Joe enjoyed the time he got to spend with his family, and I know they felt at ease knowing he would recover even though he had a long road ahead.

After a couple of days, Joe was able to progress to solid foods although his appetite was small, and things didn't taste right. Also, when he chewed, it hurt the fractures in his face. He was getting regular breathing treatments for his lungs. His vision was blurry; he had headaches; and his shoulder hurt where his clavicle was fractured. He had to keep his arm in a sling. He also had a wound vac on his stomach where his incision was. Once he was able to take a shower and shave he started looking more like himself.

Joe had speech therapy and physical therapy on a regular basis. In fact, he was able to be transferred to the physical therapy unit right there at Centerpoint. It was great to see his progress. I had returned to work that week but still stopped by in the morning and afternoon every day. I was always there for his evening meal, and we would end up watching *Family Feud* together. I would leave at 9:00 P.M. after making sure he was tucked in for the night.

Joe was so sweet to me while he was in the hospital. He seemed to be genuinely glad to have me around. He would perk up when I walked into the room. Sometimes he would get frustrated though, because with his head injury, he had poor short-term memory and would have a hard time communicating his thoughts.

When he got released to come home on August 10th, I was more than happy to welcome him with open arms. Because he needed assistance, he couldn't return to the Santa Fe house. By now we had lived apart for six months. I was certain that Joe's life was spared, because God was giving our marriage a second chance. I prayed for Joe to want to be there with me and be glad he was home, but I had the feeling that his heart was still at the Santa Fe house. It was crushing.

I took the next two weeks off work to make sure he made it downtown to his outpatient therapy since he couldn't drive. I did everything in my power to assist him and make him comfortable at home. He still had a lot of pain in his shoulder and had dizzy spells and problems with his vision. He seemed emotionally detached, but what else was new with Joe? I was just trying to do the best I could to be a support system for him.

Joe was still unable to drive, so he had been having me take him to the Santa Fe house, so he could spend time there. He actually told me he thought the reason he survived his accident was so he could finish the work he had started on the house. I quickly realized he was so consumed with that place that that's where he wanted to be. It really hurt me, because I didn't understand why he couldn't be happy at home with me.

Once he was released to drive and was back at work, I would find him going there instead of coming home. He was taking showers there and doing laundry and changing the sheets on the bed. He was even stocking the house with groceries. And he would brag when his "buddies" would stop by like it was the greatest thing in the world. I was trying to be patient, but I didn't understand.

He didn't want to be at home with me, and it hurt. I felt so rejected and didn't know what to do. The distance between us was more obvious than ever. I was beginning to wonder, since he was back at work, if he had started talking to the other woman again. By mid-November I had purchased a GPS car tracker. I figured if he was going to slip up, it would be during the day, so I placed it under his work truck. I have to admit I felt pretty sneaky, and it made me uneasy. I was essentially setting him up to fail, but if he had nothing to hide, then the laugh was on me. Right?

It only took three business days, and he was spotted at her house at 7:45 A.M. When confronted, he lied to me about his whereabouts. When I told him I knew where he had been, he told me he went there to fix her toilet.

At this point, why he was there didn't matter. The fact he was there at all shows he still couldn't be trusted. I didn't want to go down this path with them again. They had no morals or ethics, and even if nothing happened that day, it was just a matter of time, and I wasn't willing to stick around for another blind sight. I boxed all his things and put them on the doorstep at the Santa Fe house.

On my drive to work every day, I would pass Brookwood Village Townhomes and envision myself living there. As things got increasingly worse with Joe, I knew I wanted to move to Blue Springs to be closer to my job. The morning that Joe was at her house, I was so upset that I had to leave work early. I mentally couldn't function. My whole belief system in my husband was gone at this point, and his lies had really done a number on me.

When I left work that day, I immediately went to Brookwood Village and spoke with the office manager. I specifically wanted a unit with a basement, and she told me there would be an opening in January, so I left with an application in my hand. Isaiah, Hera, and I filled out all the required paperwork, and within a matter of days, we were approved.

I told Joe I was going to move to Blue Springs, sell the house, and file for divorce. Thanksgiving was just a few days away, and it would be the last one we had in that house as a family. Between Thanksgiving and Christmas, Joe turned on his charm and became Mr. Nice Guy. I was getting the best of him, because we weren't living together, and I was planning to move.

We had Jerimie and Amanda and the kids over on Christmas Eve and celebrated Christmas morning with Koen and Isaiah. It was definitely bittersweet. Once we got through the holidays, it was time to start packing. I told myself it was the right thing to do. I continued to put my trust in the Lord. I knew He had a plan for my future even though I was stepping into the unknown.

2019

Joe talked to me about wanting to stay together and try to work things out. He couldn't understand why I would move out of the Hanthorn house since he was still paying the mortgage, as if I just woke up one morning and decided to make life hard on myself.

I tried to explain to Joe that it wasn't okay for us to live apart and for him to continue to have his wife on one side of town and his girlfriend on the other. I would rather work a second job and pay my own way than to live that way. I told him the only way we could ever stay together is if he could build trust with me and find Jesus.

The big moving day was Friday, January 18th. I hired movers to come by in the afternoon in which Joe actually paid half of the fee. The only concern I had was the weather. It was cold, and there was supposed to be blizzard conditions. Joe came over after he got off work and stayed with me the first two nights in my new place. He helped me put beds together, hook up the washer and dryer, and hang things on the wall, stuff like that.

Isaiah and Hera were both working at Dairy Queen at the time, and Isaiah had just started subbing for the Blue Springs School District doing custodial work. It was nice to be able to have him fill in for me when I needed a day off work on occasion.

Koen was working at Cerner Corporation at the help desk, answering troubleshooting calls. Cerner is an American supplier of health information technology solutions, services, devices, and hardware. Its headquarters are in the suburb of North Kansas City, Missouri. He was also dating Alonso, a sweet guy from Peru.

Joe and I would spend weekends at the Hanthorn house trying to get it cleaned up and ready to sell. We both still had so much stuff in the house that we either didn't want or need that we decided to have a big garage sale. It was a difficult time, emptying out a house I loved but ultimately couldn't keep. I knew I had to follow through in order to be able to move on.

Moving on has proved to be a difficult process for me. Even though I had moved to Blue Springs and was literally two minutes from work, I didn't feel like I was any better off emotionally. We made it through another Valentine's Day, our twenty-first anniversary and my forty-eighth birthday. But nothing was different or better. Now I was just farther away, still feeling lonely and the need to distance myself.

The problem with distancing myself from Joe was he had a knack for bridging that gap and making me feel like we were going to get through this turmoil together, even though he was the reason things were falling apart to begin with. He had me convinced that I would eventually be with him at the Santa Fe house, and I wanted that so badly. He was going to expand the kitchen and give me the upstairs space to decorate however I wanted. I had allowed myself to daydream about being there with him someday. I had let Joe work his way back into my heart.

I would get off work on Friday and come home to pack a bag for the weekend. Sometimes Joe would come to my place, but the majority of the time I stayed with him. It didn't matter to me what we were doing as long as we were together. I would mostly just hang out there with him while he worked on the house. It was an investment of my time, but the problem with that is I was giving up the things I liked to do in order to be there with Joe.

I would find myself skipping my workouts at Planet Fitness or not attending church on Sunday mornings. I had been bouncing back and forth between EastSide Baptist Church and First Baptist Church of Blue Springs and was interested in finding a new church home and wanted Joe to be a part of that process with me. I thought that if we got involved with a church together then we would have a real shot at making the marriage work. I knew that if our marriage had any hope of surviving we needed God as our solid foundation.

Carrie and Jessi attended Abundant Life in Lee's Summit with their families. Carrie invited me to attend with them in December of 2018. I went twice and enjoyed hearing Pastor Phil preach but didn't want to commit myself to attending church with my sisters, because I was still holding out on the prospect that Joe would change his mind and we would find something together.

The first part of April, Joe and I took a trip to Mississippi. Joe's Aunt Faye passed away, so we went down there to attend her funeral. It gave us a good opportunity to get away and visit with family that we haven't seen in many years. It also gave me a chance to see one of my best friends, Nona Russell. Nona is married to Joe's cousin Charlie, and they are really good people. They put us up for a couple of nights, and we had a wonderful time catching up with them. Nona's one of those friends that no matter how much time goes by, we don't skip a beat; we can pick up right where we left off. I miss her and wish we lived closer. She is the epitome of Southern hospitality.

We were in the process of selling the Hanthorn house to our next-door neighbor's grandson. He was working out the details of securing his loan which was a real blessing to us. We didn't even have to put the house on the market, and we had a buyer. Only God could orchestrate that!

It was the Thursday before Easter, and I had picked Jess up for the weekend. We were at Joe's house, when out of the blue, I intercepted a text message from the other woman. I don't remember the context, but I can tell you my reaction was off the hook. Whenever this other woman was concerned, my heart would start to race, and I would get super anxious and start shaking. I told him I wasn't going to put up with it and left with Jess, so we didn't get to address the situation that evening.

This was the first time since November that she resurfaced. Maybe she's been around the whole time and I was just too naïve to notice, or maybe I was trying to be forgiving. I didn't know; I was just so confused. For months I had been giving him the benefit of the doubt. He claimed nothing was going on between them but all the lying and cheating came rushing back to me.

It turned out to be a busy weekend. Karlie spent the night on Friday, and since it was nice, the girls got to play outside. We ate pizza for dinner, colored Easter eggs, watched a movie, and snacked on candy and popcorn. Karlie had two soccer games on Saturday that we attended. Joe had a friend that was preaching on Easter Sunday, so we took Jess to church with us.

There was a strain between Joe and I, because once again, I felt the need to put my guard up. After returning Jess home that Sunday evening, I didn't talk to Joe for a few days. I felt like my paranoia was justified because of the past but the problem this time was that Joe didn't understand why I was upset, which was a problem of its own.

If there's a problem, and you can't see there's a problem, that's a problem. It boggles my mind that he thought he could be friends with this other woman, and it shouldn't affect me. I felt like I was still investing so much in the relationship with nothing in return. I was mentally and emotionally exhausted, and I felt myself spiraling downward and didn't know what to do.

It was Mother's Day weekend, Thursday, May 9th, and Susan, my mom, and I were on our way to State Recognition Days (SRD). SRD is an annual TOPS Convention meant to motivate and inspire different chapters all over the state of Missouri. This year we were headed to Springfield, and it was due to be a big weekend.

I was graduating, because I had reached my KOPS goal. I was expected to walk across the stage to accept my diploma wearing a graduation cap and black formal dress. I was also crowned Chapter Queen for MO 0331 Independence for losing the most weight in my division. And my mom was being recognized for placing second in her division and would be giving her speech to hundreds of attendees. She was nervous but did an amazing job. Robert even came down on Saturday to show her his support. I was so proud of her.

On our way to the convention, my mom was in the passenger seat and I was sitting in the back. I had laid my book down and was listening to their conversation about Susan's ex-husband being a narcissist, and it got my attention. I had heard of the word "narcissist" before, but I didn't have a clue what it meant so I picked up my phone and googled the definition: *narcissist, noun, a person who has an excessive interest in or admiration of themselves: narcissists who think the world revolves around them.*

I couldn't believe it! After reading the definition and the symptoms of narcissistic behavior, I realized for the first time that I was married to someone that fit this description perfectly. As I started reading the list of symptoms, a lot of Joe's characteristic traits started making sense after years of living with him.

— Lacking Empathy
— Dominates Conversations
— Self-importance
— False Image Projection
— Rule Breaking
— Strives for Perfection
— Charming
— Manipulation
— Desire for Control
— Blame
— Troubled Relationships

Each symptom came with a description, and I realized for the first time in my married life that there was a name for what I've been living with. I always thought Joe had PTSD or multiple personalities or something. An outsider might take a look at this same list and be completely unaware at how harmful these symptoms can be, but if you have lived with someone that suffers from NPD, then you know these symptoms are a brew for a very toxic relationship.

It was at this time that I began doing a lot of research on NPD. It gave me a real understanding as to why things were the way they were and better yet, why it was so hard for me to break free from this cycle. It is said that people that suffer from NPD can sustain a relationship, but the other person is often left with unmet expectations and/or feelings of emptiness.

I got home that Saturday evening and remember missing church the next day because I didn't want to be the only mother sitting alone on Mother's Day. Isaiah had to work, so I made plans to have dinner with Koen, Alonso, and Alonso's mom and dad. His parents were already in town from Peru, because Alonso graduated the day before. It was nice to meet them even though they don't speak much English. Alonso had to translate the conversation. It was very interesting to say the least.

We closed on the Hanthorn house in June. It was great timing, because it allowed me to get a few bills paid off and put some money in the bank.

It's a tradition to go to BoBo's house on the Fourth of July. The whole family was there which meant good company, delicious food, and fireworks. I cut out a bit early to go over to Joe's. Isaiah and Hera showed up along with Jerimie, Amanda, and the grandkids. We had a really good time.

After the party died down and everyone went home, I crawled into bed and snuggled under the covers. Joe had put his phone on the charger and got in the shower. Things had been going well with us lately, and he genuinely seemed happy to have me around that evening. I decided to look at his phone, so I picked it up and put his four-digit code in, and there it was, another message from "what's her name."

I immediately got out of bed and started to get dressed when Joe walked into the room. I confronted him, and he actually tried to be dismissive like he had no idea how those messages got on his phone or why she would have texted him to begin with. He begged me to stay, tried to minimize my reaction, and insisted it was nothing. But I couldn't stay. The rejection I felt was more than I could bear. Why couldn't he just stop?

I was always holding out hope that she would eventually become a thing of the past, that each encounter with her would be the last. I know the outside world might not understand my warped sense of reality, but to me, Joe was my world. I had put so much of myself into him that at times I felt as if I had truly lost my identity. Who was Heather? Did she even exist at all?

At the end of July my mom and I took a little trip to Eureka Springs, Arkansas. It was a much-needed getaway. We stayed at a bed-and-breakfast called Red Bud Manor. It was simply delightful. Our first stop in town was at Keels Creek Winery where I sampled and purchased a couple bottles of zinfandel. I enjoy a good glass of wine on occasion.

Later that evening we stopped at a little Italian restaurant for dinner on our way to the Crescent Hotel where we experienced a haunted tour. We didn't witness any ghosts or spirits but found it to be "eerie" just the same and were very interested in the overall history of the hotel.

Mom and I had so much fun, we stayed an extra night on a whim. We toured Quigley's Castle (Ozarks strangest dwelling) as well as watched *The Great Passion Play*. We had a fabulous time shopping, sightseeing, and eating some really fabulous food.

Joe and I along with Jerimie, Amanda, Isaiah, and Hera had plans to attend a tribute concert at the Providence Medical Center Amphitheater, commonly known as Sandstone, in Bonner Springs, Kansas. With everything going on with Joe, it had been a couple of weeks since I talked to him but decided to make this a family event.

So, upon my return from Eureka Springs, I stopped at Joe's house. Isaiah and Hera came over, and we rode to the concert together. Jerimie and Amanda met us there. We ended up having a wonderful time. Of course, Joe wooed me back into his good graces, and I let him. We lay under the stars, holding hands, and I ended up spending the night with him.

My mom and I decided that we wanted to start our own TOPS chapter, but in order to do so, we had to meet certain requirements. We had to have a minimum of four members. We were lucky enough to start with five. Our members included myself, my mom, my cousin Susan, and Sheila. We were all transfers from MO 0331 Independence. We also had my Aunt Deanie, Susan's mom (and my gram's sister) who transferred from MO 0100 Independence.

We had to have a meeting place, and it just so happened that my mom's pastor agreed to let us meet at their church, Southview Baptist, in Raytown. That gave us a place to have a room to hold our weekly meetings. We also had to have a set of scales so we could conduct our weekly "weigh-ins" for each member. The scales needed to have their own room for privacy purposes. Ironically enough, Robert was able to acquire medical scales from the elementary school nurse's office that he works for. They were getting new scales, so it worked out great for us.

We had to have assigned officers. I was the leader of my previous chapter, so it made sense that I resumed that role. Deanie was our weight recorder and Susan our treasurer in which they both had experience, and Sheila was our secretary. My mom became co-leader (from the previous chapter) and assistant weight recorder, so we had all of our required officers in place.

There was a bunch of paperwork to be filled out, including transfer forms and weight charts, and we needed to open a bank account. Delight Davis, our advocate for Missouri chapters, had to be present for our very first meeting which we decided would be held on Thursday evenings. So, on August 8, 2019 Chapter MO 1338 Raytown was born. Everything just fell into place, as if it was meant to be. Another blessing from God.

It's awesome to be part of a support group and encourage each other (and be encouraged) weekly. We love it, and we're excited to grow our chapter as we add new members.

This year kicked off the 2019 – 2020 school year. It's always great to get back into the swing of things and see staff and students after the summer break. Every once in a while, administrators will get transferred to a different school. I was fond of Dr. Flax and had a lot of respect for him, and I was genuinely sad to see him go.

It just so happened that Casey Brownsberger was offered a principal position within the Blue Springs School District after being an assistant for years. Remember, Casey was Jan Castle's assistant in 2014, the year I was hired at Franklin Smith. Luckily for me (and the staff as a whole) she got permanent placement right there at James Walker. It was a great fit, since she was there the year before and had a good rapport with the staff and students. It was a plus that her and I already had a good working relationship.

I was particularly excited to see my good friend Rhonda Littrell. Rhonda manages the kitchen at JWE, and her and I have gotten close over the two years that I've worked there. She's the one person that I've been able to confide in about my personal life. In fact, most days she knew something was wrong with me before I ever said anything.

Rhonda and I took a few minutes to catch up. Her husband Greg had been struggling with some health issues and had passed away a few months earlier in May. I knew her loss was still fresh, but she has a great family support system, so it was good to see she was getting along well.

Of course, Rhonda asked me how things were going with Joe. She knew of our on-again, off-again relationship, so it didn't surprise her that nothing much had changed. I even joked around with her once and told her she's probably getting tired of hearing about all of my problems. All Rhonda said was "No matter what, I'm here for you." She has been a true friend and trusted confidant.

Ironically enough, about a week into the school year, I came across more text messages on Joe's phone. This time the other woman implied that she'd been at the Santa Fe house. Joe tried to convince me that nothing was going on and that she was crazy. I believed the part about her being crazy. Who else goes after a married man for over two years and acts like his wife is the one with a problem? I know I gave Joe more than enough chances, but he was MY husband. She had no right to him, no matter what lies he was telling her. I finally just started calling her a homewrecker, even though Joe was just as much to blame, if not more.

Some of her other text messages were just too personal. For example, she knew that we had gone to a concert together and I stayed the night with him. And she was concerned that he might be intimate with me (of course her verbiage was very vulgar), and that if he was, that was a deal breaker for her. Seriously? She just knew too much, and there was no way Joe could talk his way out of it anymore. I knew that all the times I had caught him in a lie that there were probably ten more times that I didn't. He was out of chances.

I told Joe it was time to follow through with divorce. I had dragged my feet and put it off as long as I could just hoping he would change his ways. I fought this outcome to the bitter end.

There were moments that I felt like I was even rebelling against God. As much time as I've spent in prayer over my husband and my marriage, God revealed to me more than enough indiscretions that are grounds for divorce. I know God is against divorce, but I also know God gives us free will, and Joe chose over and over again to go against his marriage vows.

I was in tears the day I walked into the attorney's office and turned over divorce papers that I was holding on to from one year earlier.

It was Friday, August 30th, Labor Day weekend, and I stopped by the attorney's office to sign my petition for divorce. I was overwhelmed with emotion. I was extremely sad, but I also felt a tremendous amount of guilt. I felt guilty, because I thought I was giving up on Joe and, in theory, giving up on us. My heart broke for a man that I knew deep in my heart loves me but would rather risk losing me over his own selfish desires. He never thought I would follow through with divorce, and he played it out as long as he could. I was reminded that day in Philippians 4:13 that says, "I can do all things through Christ who strengthens me."

I had made arrangements with Joe to bring his part of the legal document from the attorney's office to his house. We were going to take it to the bank to be signed and notarized, but he already had an eye appointment at the mall that evening. So, in typical Joe fashion, he asked me to go to the mall with him, and we would go to the bank in the morning. I agreed, of course, and we ended up at Olive Garden for dinner. Go figure!

Later that evening, while watching a movie on the couch, we both ended up falling asleep before it was over, so we just went to bed. I was awakened at 1:00 A.M. with quite a bit of discomfort. At first I thought maybe I had eaten too much pasta and breadsticks at dinner, because I had been limiting my carbs. By 4:00 A.M. I knew something was seriously wrong, because I was in so much pain. I had Joe take me to the emergency room at Centerpoint Hospital.

We were at the hospital for about three hours from the time we arrived to the time we left. I went through a CAT scan and an ultrasound before it was determined that I had kidney stones. There's a first time for everything. If you've ever experienced kidney stones, then you know the pain I'm talking about, and if you haven't, consider yourself lucky!

Joe was very sweet and patient, feeding me ice chips and making sure I was comfortable. Once the doctor administered some pain meds and I was able to relax a bit, I remember looking across the room at Joe, and the only thing I was thinking was "we have to get those divorce papers signed."

After we left the hospital, Joe stopped at Walgreens to pick up my prescription, and then we went to McDonald's for a breakfast sandwich. He graciously let me sleep in his bed all day long. During that time, Joe took the document to the bank and had it notarized. He made sure I was fed, taken care of, and medicated. I finally passed the kidney stone at 10:00 P.M. that evening. What a relief.

It's the end of September, and I've had a few really good weeks with Joe, even though divorce was looming. He was acting like everything was going to be fine, maybe even better. Narcissists live in a fantasy world in which this was a clear sign that Joe couldn't accept the reality that we were indeed getting a divorce. In most cases, when you file for divorce, you move on. That was the problem with our relationship. Neither one of us knew how to successfully move on. We couldn't figure out how to let each other go.

The bottom line for me at this point is trust, or lack of. I had to put my car in the shop for a couple of days, so Joe let me borrow his truck. I took this opportunity to re-activate that fancy little GPS tracking device. I figured no harm, no foul. I mean, if Joe was still pursuing me and making me feel as if we still had a chance, why not test his trust.

I installed the tracker on Wednesday and returned his truck to him on Thursday. By Friday, Joe already piqued my interest. As I was sitting in the comfort of my own home, I noticed he was at Centerpoint Hospital via the GPS app on my cell phone. Curious as I was, I got in my car and drove there. I positioned my car in the parking lot, so I had a clear view of his truck and waited.

About forty-five minutes later I saw two people walking towards his vehicle, him and her. I've seen Joe with this woman on several different occasions, and each time, my blood boils. I followed him to the opposite side of the parking lot and that wench was already standing next to his opened passenger door. As I whipped my car alongside Joe's truck, the look on his face was priceless. He couldn't believe I just showed up out of the clear blue. As soon as she saw me, she headed for her car and ducked inside just in time for me to pick up an orange construction cone and wail it in her direction.

Joe proceeded to tell me that her mom was in the hospital, in which I replied, "Who cares?" I mean seriously, why was he there? He's not part of her family. I was angry, because Joe took an opportunity to spend time with this woman when he thought I was occupied for the night. Integrity means the quality of being honest and having strong moral principles which implies doing the right thing, even when nobody's watching. Joe does what he wants to, and he doesn't think about the consequences or the people he hurts along the way.

I was not going to compete for a place next to Joe, and he proved over and over again that he couldn't be trusted. I was sad, and my heart was broken, again. This ultimately confirmed to me that divorce was absolutely the right decision. I drove away from Joe that evening and went home, glad to have a place of my own.

Psalm 46:1 says, "God is our refuge and strength, an ever-present help in trouble." The reality is that there will be difficult times, but God promises to be our refuge. I'm so very thankful that I have my faith to rely on in times of need.

I didn't talk to Joe for a week, and when I did, he was getting ready to take a trip to Colorado. It was Friday, October 4th, and it was Joe's last day at work. He finally made it to retirement and was ready to hit the road. He asked me to drive out there with him, but I just couldn't. I tend to wear my feelings on my sleeve, and I knew I wouldn't be able to see his family and pretend everything was okay. His birthday was the following Sunday, so he was able to celebrate with his two sisters, brother, nieces, and nephews. He hadn't seen his family since his accident, so everybody was happy to see each other.

Joe and I continued to talk every day. We were even still seeing each other on the weekends. Things were plugging along, not at all like we were in the process of getting a divorce. Although this was his pattern, it gave me mixed messages. It's like Joe didn't want me, but he wanted to "keep" me, but only on his terms. That was his way of always being in control, and it took an emotional toll on me. I was with Joe for twenty-five years, and I was conditioned to this mentality.

This led to feelings of rejection, failure, and insignificance. There were times I felt physical pain. I wondered what was wrong with me and why wasn't I good enough. How could Joe be so content living in that house without me? It was my dream too. Didn't he miss my presence? I did everything I could, and I still didn't measure up.

On Monday, November 12th, we both walked into the attorney's office and signed final papers to dissolve our marriage.

Exactly one week later, on November 18th, I received an email from my attorney saying I was officially divorced. Just like that, twenty-one years gone (I actually opened the email on Isaiah's twenty-first birthday). Even though I was expecting it, the news brought me to my knees. I couldn't believe it really happened. I called Joe immediately. I was crying when he answered the phone, and he was consoling me, telling me he was sorry and things were going to be okay. I was still turning to him for love and comfort when he's been the cause for so much of my pain and suffering.

I was completely broken and overwhelmed with emotion. I was sad for a marriage that was lost. I was sad, because I had given everything to Joe, and he let me go without a fight. I was sad, because when he had me, he didn't want me. I was sad, because there was no more "us."

The depression worsened. There were times I didn't know how I was going to get out of bed in the morning. I would open my eyes and ask God to give me the strength to make it through the day.

I think loneliness has affected me the most. One of the things I valued about being married was having a constant companion, my best friend. I enjoyed waking up to Joe and talking over coffee. I looked forward to seeing my husband when I got home from work. And even though we never really did have a healthy relationship, I sure missed having him around. We've been separated for so long that I've actually gotten used to sleeping alone and having meals alone and watching movies alone, but I don't enjoy the solitude day in and day out.

At the end of the month, we decided to have Thanksgiving dinner at the Santa Fe house since my townhouse wouldn't accommodate everybody. Joe put two six-foot tables end on end to seat all of us, and I cooked the same meal that I did every year.

Joseph and Tim joined us along with Jerimie, Amanda, Karlie, and Noah. Kevanah was with her mom that year. We also had Koen, Alonso, Isaiah, and Hera. The meal itself was good, but on a personal level, it just felt plain awkward. We were legally divorced, and it was like we were trying to go through the motions. I told myself it would be our last Thanksgiving Day together as a family unit.

We made it through December without any surprises from the other woman. Joe and I went to Jerimie and Amanda's house to celebrate on Christmas Eve. Amanda's mom, two sisters, and baby nephew were in town. We ate dinner and had an enjoyable evening with everyone. After that, I spent the night with Joe, and we woke up on Christmas morning and exchanged our gifts.

Later that day, Joe joined me at my house while we celebrated with Koen, Alonso, Isaiah, and Hera. My cat, Jasper, was part of the festivities too. He always had to be the center of attention especially if wads of wrapping paper were involved. We had brunch and opened presents just like every other year. Koen commented later that he was surprised to see Joe there, and I just shrugged it off.

Sticking with tradition, I joined the rest of my family at Jessi and Mario's house later that evening. I had a good time, but deep down, I was very sad. My head and my heart were battling it out. I knew I had to figure out a way to let Joe go but was still so much connected to him. I was really suffering internally.

We got to pick up our Princess Jess the following Friday for the weekend. The funny thing is she is more of a "tomboy" than a "princess," but she'll always be a princess to me. As usual, it was great to see her sweet face. She opened her gifts, and I got her the wrong Vans, so on Saturday, she and I went to the mall, so she could pick out a pair she liked. We met up with Joe later on that evening and picked up Karlie and saw *Jumanji* in the theater. On Monday, Jess and I had lunch with my mom, and we went to the movies again. This time we saw *Little Women*. We had a great time.

I told Jess that weekend that Joe and I were divorced. It made her sad, and we both cried, but I explained to her that our divorce would never interfere with our relationship with her and that we both loved her very much. I also told Jess that this was a new year, a new millennium, and a new Heather! Even though we chuckled at my remark, I knew in my heart that I was going to have to dig deep down to make some pretty significant changes in the year to come.

2020

I decided to stay home on New Year's Eve. I just didn't feel like Joe and I had anything to celebrate, so while Jerimie, Amanda, and the kids went to his house, I watched a movie alone and was in bed before midnight. I couldn't believe it had been two years since I found out about Joe's affair.

So much had happened since then. In 2019 I moved into my own place, we sold our house on Hanthorn, and got divorced. I was bound and determined that this year was going to be better. It was time for me to find happiness for myself and finally learn how to heal.

I chose the word "hope" for my 2020 word of the year. Romans 15:13 tells us "May the God of Hope fill you with <u>joy</u> and <u>peace</u> as you <u>trust</u> in Him, so that you may overflow with hope by the power of the Holy Spirit." Unbenounced to me at the time, I chose this scripture to accompany the word hope that God had woven together my last three years-worth of words into one verse. A coincidence? I think not.

Carrie told me that Abundant Life Baptist Church in Lee's Summit was opening a brand-new campus in Blue Springs. Their very first kick-off service was on January 5th, and I was eager to attend. I had already been trying to put a distance between Joe and I with fewer overnight visits. I told him that I would no longer be staying at his house on Saturday night, because I was going to be in church every Sunday morning from here on out.

The minute I walked through the doors at Abundant Life in Blue Springs, I felt like I was at home. I had been looking for a church to attend for two years, and the feeling I got was overwhelming. I recognized people I knew from previous churches and places of employment and couldn't believe how connected I felt after just one time attending.

Phil Hopper has been the pastor of Abundant Life for twenty years. He obviously couldn't be in two places at once, so while he was preaching at the pulpit in Lee's Summit, there was a live stream that reached all of us in Blue Springs. It was amazing! The screen went from the bottom of the stage all the way to the ceiling, so we got to see all of him. It was just like he was walking around on the stage preaching right there in front of us.

Of course, Blue Springs had their own worship team, so we got to really feel the presence of the Lord with a live worship leader and musicians. I was extremely proud to see my nephew Nate, Jessi's son, on stage playing the guitar.

I left church that day hungry for more. I loved how Pastor Phil bridged the gap and spoke of bringing the "Summit" to the "Springs" and the community that would be reached after purchasing the space a whole year earlier. He also spoke of the construction required to transform it from a gym to a church. (Ironically, I had been employed there when it was formerly Club 7 Fitness back in 2011.)

I went home and immediately registered for the Dinner with the Pastors, which is scheduled on a monthly basis, to meet some of the different pastors on staff. The dinner I attended was held on Sunday, February 9th, and there were about 140 people present. It was the first dinner offered at the Blue Springs Campus with an overwhelming turn out.

Both of my sisters and their husbands were hosts for the dinner. That meant they sat at a table to help lead the conversations and be available to answer any questions that one might have. I got reacquainted with a nice couple that Joe and I went to EastSide with, and we ended up sitting at Jessi and Mario's table. It was a very pleasant and enjoyable evening.

It was suggested at the dinner to register for the Next Steps classes which would be starting on March 1st. Next Steps is meant to give you an understanding about membership at Abundant Life with an opportunity to learn the churches mission, vision, and core values. Jessi encouraged me to sign up for the classes, because it's better to get started now rather than let a lot of time go by. So, I went home and got myself signed up.

Pastor Phil wrote a book titled *The Weapons of our Warfare* and was available to purchase at church. Jessi bought me a copy out of the kindness of her heart, and I appreciated that so much. *The Weapons of our Warfare* was going to be Pastor Phil's sermon series for the next few weeks, so I was anxious to start reading the book right away. I soon realized that, for so many years, I was a lukewarm Christian with one foot in and one foot out. I would go to church on Sundays, which seemed to get fewer and farther between over the last couple years, but that was about it. Even though I knew I had a personal relationship with Jesus Christ, ever since I started attending Abundant Life, I felt like a new Christian all over again, eager for more.

Not only did I want to get involved with the Next Steps classes, I also had a desire to find a place within the church to volunteer or serve as well as find a Bible study to attend. At the Dinner with the Pastors, they also talked about opening up the offices with counselors which was something I was very interested in. I thought I could benefit from some counseling sessions to try and sort out some of the emotional stuff I'd been going through.

Joe came over for dinner on Valentine's Day. I made the usual chicken parmesan with breadsticks and salad. It was really good. We watched a movie, and he stayed the night. The very next day, while Joe was still there, I had a really disheartening conversation with Isaiah about church, Christianity, and faith.

You see, I took my boys to church early on. Koen was six years old when we started attending Stony Point Christian Church, the same church Joe and I got married in. Isaiah was a newborn in that church and spent time in the nursery there. As they grew, we were at church every Sunday as a family, and my kids participated in Sunday school on a weekly basis and vacation Bible school in the summer.

When we transferred our membership to First Baptist Church of Raytown, we continued going to church as a family. Joe and I got connected in a Sunday school class of our own and made sure the boys attended each week. It's also where Joe, Koen, and I got baptized. I volunteered with the Awana Program for children, so every Wednesday evening I took Isaiah to class. He worked through a book, and I helped him learn memory verses so he could earn awards and prizes, all of which he enjoyed.

When we started attending EastSide Baptist Church, Koen was still plugged into the youth program at FBR and drove himself to church each week. Joe and I once again found a Sunday school class that met directly before church on Sunday mornings, and we also got involved with a connection group that met outside of church on Sunday evenings.

Each week, we would drop Isaiah off at "kids' club," and he would play and participate in activities in the gym. Once he reached middle school and got transferred to the youth program he lost interest, so our twelve-year-old son would sit with us in our class, and then he would sit with us in the church service. That situation lasted for a couple of years, and I thought it was sufficient. At least he was hearing the word of God, right?

It was in 2012 when I started working at QuikTrip (the same time period that we bought the Peculiar house) that church got put on hold for a while, at least for me. I worked every Sunday (in the bakery), and although Joe was still attending our Sunday school class, he didn't attend regular church on Sunday mornings, and he didn't make Isaiah go as well. After only one year at QT, I started working in the warehouse, which just so happened to be closed on Sundays. By this time, my now fifteen-year-old son refused to get out of bed on Sunday mornings to go to church.

At that time, I didn't enforce Isaiah to go. For one thing, if you know Isaiah, he's very strong-willed, and it just didn't seem worth the fight, at the time. And second, I didn't think he would have benefited from sitting in church with an attitude, arms crossed, rebelling against the world. This is where as a parent it's easy to beat myself up with regret. Was it my fault that he lost interest, and was I so consumed with my own marital problems that I somehow failed my son along the way? What could I have done differently? Coulda, shoulda, woulda...

Somewhere along the way, Isaiah grew very skeptical where religion and biblical facts and timelines take place. I suppose I just thought that because I've always had faith and believed, that my children would always have faith and believe. That's how I was raised so it made sense to me that it would be the same for them, no questions asked. Although Isaiah's always known my position where my faith is concerned, I knew that he must make his own faith journey, and I couldn't force my beliefs on him. I had to turn it over to God and keep praying and wait.

Now, back to the conversation I had with Isaiah. Even though I knew of his skepticism, it wasn't until this particular moment that I realized the magnitude of it. We got on the subject of God's creation and answered prayers and heaven which is something we normally don't talk about. Isaiah's perspective is that of logic where mine is that of faith.

Isaiah expressed that he basically believes in the big bang theory (where two meteors collide) which caused earth and that everything else was made up of stardust. He proceeded to say that people like me (religious) believe when good things happen (answered prayer) it comes from God, but people like him (skeptics) believe when good things happen, it's because of their own doing. And then he told me Adam and Eve couldn't be the first human creation, because that would be incestuous, and he further told me he doesn't believe in heaven, that when people die, they just die.

I realized with this mentality I wasn't going to see Isaiah in heaven, and that immediately brought me to tears. How could this be my son's way of thinking? He wasn't raised this way.

I was right in the midst of reading Pastor Phil's book, *The Weapons of our Warfare*, and it had given me a totally different perspective on sin and defeating the enemy. I knew this was Satan's way of telling lies to my son, and the worst part was, I couldn't do or say anything to convince him otherwise. Isaiah already had his mind made up and all his "facts" against my God were stacked against me. I knew I personally couldn't disprove his beliefs, so I suggested he read a book in God's favor or talk to somebody with answers to any questions he might have. He honestly didn't think it was necessary to be convinced of anything other than what he already believes. That scared me, so I knew that the only thing I could do was turn it over to God.

Phillipians 4:6-7 tells us "Do not be anxious about anything, but in everything by prayer and supplication with thanksgiving let your requests be made known to God. And the peace of God, which surpasses all understanding, will guard your hearts and your minds in Christ Jesus."

Every day I ask the Lord to keep both of my boys, Koen and Isaiah, safe from the enemy and draw them near Him. As a mother, first and foremost, I'm glad that I have a good relationship with my adult children. I silently hand them to God, clinging to the assurance that He knows their needs, and in His time and in His way, will work it out in their lives.

I will continue to pray for Isaiah's salvation. He's an intelligent young man, and I would love to see him apply his knowledge towards God's truth, and that he will one day surrender his life to Christ. All I can do is be a witness to him by example and leave the rest to God. Ezekial 36:26 says, "I will give you a new heart and put a new spirit in you; I will remove from you your heart of stone and give you a heart of flesh."

Both Koen and Isaiah agreed to go to church with me on my birthday that was quickly approaching. I was super excited, and I prayed that God would speak to them, and His presence would be felt through Pastor Phil's sermon.

So, as it turns out, Pastor Phil was the author of not only one book but two. He was going to be at church doing a "book signing," so I made sure to order *Defeating the Enemy* (book number one) from Amazon. I got there early that morning, with both of my books in hand, ready to have them autographed.

As I approached the table and slid my books towards him, I introduced myself. I mentioned Carrie and Jessi and told Pastor Phil I was their "other" sister. As he opened the first book to sign, I proceeded to tell him how much I loved Abundant Life and felt at home immediately. I only had a moment of his time and got choked up when I spoke of my recent divorce. Upon completion of signing the second book, he graciously took my hand and lifted me up in prayer, confirming my decision to make Abundant Life my permanent church home.

I stopped by Joe's house one Thursday evening before my TOPS meeting, and we had a spontaneous conversation. I started talking to him about my faith and the fact that he decided he didn't need to go to church or have a relationship with God. It opened up a conversation that needed to be had.

I explained to Joe that attending church wasn't just something that I suggested we do together after twenty-one years of marriage but that we've always gone as a family. I told him my relationship with God was important to me, and I wanted to continue to go. That through the course of our two-year separation, before our divorce, I invited him to go to church with me on Sunday mornings multiple times and even suggested we find a different church to go to all together. Joe didn't want any part of that, so I would end up skipping church most Sundays, because I didn't want to go alone, and I was holding out hope that he would join me.

I shared with him how all through the years, when he would witness me spending time with God in prayer with scripture, that I was praying for him, for our marriage, and for our family. That when I meditated over my word of the year, in particular acceptance, that I was asking God that I could "accept" Joe for the unique person He created him to be. That even though my needs have gone unmet for years that it was never about me. It was always about loving Joe regardless of how difficult our marriage had been.

I explained to Joe that even through his mood swings, bitter, angry attitude, refusing affection, denying me intimacy, not wearing his wedding ring, and never saying the words "I love you" over the years, that I would have stayed, because he was my husband and all I ever wanted was for "us" to always try to work it out. Because I was already there, already his wife, I was willing to stick it out and obey my wedding vows no matter what.

But as soon as infidelity was brought into our marriage, that was something I would never be able to accept or compromise on nor should I. No sooner did he move into the Santa Fe house did he start bringing the other woman there, the home that was bought with the intention that we would fix it up together and someday live there. He tarnished that for me. It was no longer our place; it was Joe's place. And even though I still had a glimmer of hope that one day I would join him there, before the divorce, there was absolutely no effort made on his part to reconcile our differences.

I was resisting divorce so much that it was as if I was digging my heels into the ground, skidding to a halt. I expressed to him how terrifying it was for me to move to the townhouse, but that after so much time apart, with no changes to the relationship, I was basically forced to follow through with threats to move to Blue Springs, sell the home I loved, and file for divorce.

I was able to ask Joe why it was so hard for him to be intimate with me over the years and his reply was, "it was too personal". That actually rang true for me. What I longed for the most from my husband was the hardest for him to give. It was easier for him to give it to somebody else because there was no emotion involved; it was meaningless. He was fulfilling a selfish desire with somebody he didn't have to have an emotional attachment to. To finally be able to recognize this brought clarity. All the way back to our first anniversary when he told me I wasn't good, was his way of detaching himself. I believe Joe never meant to intentionally hurt me but because he lacks empathy he couldn't grasp the magnitude of the pain caused. But that doesn't excuse it. I spent years thinking it was me, not understanding, but now it makes sense. It wasn't me at all.

I told Joe how much I loved Abundant Life, the church I had been attending for the past six weeks. My faith is not something new; it's been a reflection of my whole life and being there on Sunday mornings was absolutely where I was called to be. The presence of the Lord consumed me and rocked me to the core. I knew I had found my church home. I shared this with Joe and told him I had attended the "Dinner with the Pastors," that I registered for the "Next Steps" classes, because I wanted to become a member of the church. I told him I wanted to get involved in a bible study as well as start to serve/volunteer.

I also mentioned Christian counseling, because I didn't know how to let Joe go, and we sat and cried together, because he didn't know how to let me go either. It was sad. But I told him that we just wanted different things in life, and because there was so much water under the bridge, we couldn't go back. I knew Satan had an emotional stronghold on me. With some counseling, I knew I could work on being whole and healthy for the next phase in my life.

We talked about his Narcissistic Personality Disorder and how much that has played a part in our marriage, because he doesn't know how to be in a healthy relationship.

I told Joe that somewhere down the road I wanted to be remarried, because I value the marriage relationship. I desire having a companion, someone to share life with, someone that wants to see me every day and not live without me, someone to come home to after work and eat meals with and vacation with and is proud to wear their wedding ring and wouldn't think of taking it off. Someone that I can trust and that wants to be intimate with me and that respects me and my feelings, because my feelings do matter. And most important, someone that loves God, because if they love God, they will love me.

I left Joe's house that night feeling relieved that I was able to express to him what was going on within me even though I still found myself feeling overcome by guilt at times. Guilt because I had somehow given up on him. I know all of the good qualities Joe possesses, and I truly loved him, and I know he loved me the best way he knew how. I would have gone to the end of the Earth for him, and sometimes it felt like I did. I always thought he was worth the fight, but there came a point in time when I realized love just wasn't enough.

After attending Abundant Life and hearing Pastor Phil preach and reading his book, *The Weapons of our Warfare* I realized without a shadow of a doubt what I was up against. For twenty-one years, I was fighting spiritual warfare within my marriage, and our marriage was an easy target.

My prayers alone weren't enough. A marriage needs to be built with God as the foundation, or it will crack and crumble to the ground before your very eyes. Joe and I didn't have solid ground. We were fighting a battle for years and didn't even know it. I had given up so much of myself, but I refused to compromise where my faith was concerned.

I had come off a weekend where I spent too much time with Joe. We ate tacos at his house on Friday night following a movie, and I found myself back over there Sunday evening for a cook-out. The weather was nice, so Joe had Jerimie, Amanda, and the kids there. Isaiah and Hera came over as well.

It's obvious I'm still in Joe's clutches. It was a Monday morning, and I woke up with feelings of unmet expectations, inadequacy, failure, rejection, and guilt. Normally, I would go about my day feeling depressed, as if life is getting the best of me, but after finishing *Defeating the Enemy*, I'm aware that these are nothing more than Satan's lies. He wants me to feel worthless. He wants to bait me, so I fall into his trap and ultimately that bait will become my bondage.

When we begin to covet things, it's a sin. It's not a sin to want something until that something becomes an idol. For example, Joe has always been a hard worker and it's a great quality to have, but when it becomes your main source of security, it becomes idolatry. Even though he's retired, all he wants to do is work, work, work. All he thinks about is his next project; it consumes him.

A while back, my mom told me that she thought much of my happiness depends on Joe. It occurred to me that for so many years I've made Joe my source of security, in turn, making him my idol. Satan knows our area of brokenness and customizes the bait for his victims.

When we allow ourselves to live in bondage, whatever it may be, we're giving Satan that stronghold. He knows our place of idolatry, but what I've learned from Pastor Phil is that we are "free to flee." And Paul tells us in 1 Corinthians 10:14, "Therefore, my dear friends, flee from idolatry."

When I set Joe free (my idol) I will essentially set myself free. My heart and my head seem to be in a constant battle. I know there is no future for Joe and me. My "head" tells me he's right where he wants to be, living in a house that was supposed to be ours, working himself to the bone, fixing it up while he clearly prefers single life over married life.

The more time I spend with him over there, the harder it is on my "heart," because it's a place where he's content without me. The reality is, nothing's changed for Joe. He has me exactly where he wants me, available with no strings attached. Anybody can be a nice guy and turn on the charm one day a week.

March 1st was the first of four Next Steps classes to be held Sunday morning during the first church service. My niece, Brooklyn, Jessi's daughter, would also be attending. I thought it was neat to be going through the classes together. Abundant Life's mission is "To see lives changed by Jesus" and their vision is "To be living proof of a loving God to a watching world." In the four-week sessions, we would be covering their six core values which are worship, evangelism, generosity, serving, discipleship, and community.

Our first week, we focused on evangelism, which is reaching people far from God. I thought that was ironic, since I just had a conversation a couple of weeks earlier with my own son. We spoke of the gospel which means "good news." Romans 6:23: "For the wages of sin is death, but the gift of God is eternal life in Christ Jesus our Lord." Sin separates us from God in this life and the next. I also learned church is not about religion; it's about a relationship.

We talked about sharing the gospel, receiving the gift of salvation and baptism. Baptism is a public confession before others and an act of confirmation. Even though I have been baptized before, I knew that I wanted to be baptized again. It was important for me to rededicate my life to the Lord. I could feel myself growing spiritually and relished in the moment. We also talked about sharing our own story of salvation. We were encouraged to go home and write a three-minute testimony outline that we could share the next week.

The following Friday was a Bible study called "single and satisfied" that I wanted to attend. It's held on the first Friday of the month in Lee's Summit at their Core Auditorium. It was five dollars at the door that paid for dinner which consisted of Minskey's Pizza and salad. It was huge for me to just walk into a place like that without knowing anybody. I was nervous, but I knew Satan would have liked it if I had just stayed home alone without trying to socialize with fellow Christians, and I wasn't going to give him that satisfaction. I went, met some new people, and had a great time.

The very next day was March 7th and would have marked our twenty-second anniversary. I was going to try to avoid Joe, because I didn't feel like we had anything to celebrate but Jess's brother had suddenly passed away, and we wanted to attend his celebration of life together so we could pay our respects to Jess and her family. It was good to visit with our girl for a little bit and see that her and her parents were doing well under the circumstances.

It was a nice day, and since the visitation was at Lake Jacomo, Joe and I drove around and went to see the elk and buffalo. Then he bought me ice cream at Andy's, and we came back to my house and visited for a while before he went home.

The next day at church was our second Next Steps class, and we talked about worship and generosity. John 4:23 says, "But the hour is coming, and now is, when the true worshipers will worship the Father in spirit and truth; for the Father is seeking such to worship Him." We worship God, because we love Him.

We learned in class that generosity and worship both have sacrifice in common. Essentially, giving is not about the size of the gift but the size of the sacrifice. Once we understand God gave us everything, we can give back to Him freely. 2 Corinthians 9:7 reminds us "God loves a cheerful giver."

Joe and I had another heart to heart conversation just a couple of days before my forty-ninth birthday. We were talking about what we should do to celebrate. We were going to go to the annual "Snake Parade" on Saturday, but they cancelled the event due to the coronavirus.

The coronavirus (COVID-19) is an infectious disease that spreads through droplets of saliva or discharge through the nose when an infected person coughs or sneezes. People that get infected will experience a respiratory illness and recover without special treatment. The people that are in danger of the disease and that could find it fatal, are the elderly or someone that may already have an underlying health problem. It originated in China and has quickly spread in multiple countries defining the virus a "pandemic." It became a health issue in the United States in the early part of March.

Joe mentioned it would be nice to take a long weekend and go to Branson, since I had Monday and Tuesday off due to spring break. We then decided it would be smart to keep it low key and not travel to avoid the chance of catching the virus or spreading it.

It was at that moment I told Joe our relationship was in no position to take little mini-vacations or road trips anymore. The investment was no longer necessary. I had given my everything and had nothing left to spare; there was no reason to keep pretending.

We stood in his kitchen and held tight to each other that evening as we cried. We cried for what was and what could have been. The truth of the matter is Joe can't change, or he would have. I've learned you cannot change a person with NPD or make them happy by loving them enough or by changing to meet their whims or desires.

Narcissists can't feel fulfilled in relationships, or in any area of their lives, because nothing is ever special enough for them. The sad reality is nobody will ever be enough for Joe, because Joe's never enough for himself. My heart breaks for the "little boy" Joe that was never held or loved as a child. I can't fix him, I know, because I've tried.

It was a big deal for Joe to tell me he really does love me and all he wants is for me to be happy. For him to say that he knows he can't meet my emotional needs and that he hopes I'll find those qualities in somebody else was what I needed to hear. Joe and I have both really struggled to let go of each other, so this was a huge weight lifted off my shoulders. It was a step in the right direction.

This was a turning point for me, because I no longer needed Joe to define myself. I am valuable in the eyes of the Lord. It was then that I knew I could truly start to heal. The cycle that I was trying to break was finally coming around.

There was nothing that could keep me away from church on Sunday mornings until the coronavirus reared its ugly head. The virus began to spread so rapidly that it quickly became a threat to society. Government officials declared it a state of emergency, therefore resulting in large gatherings to be shut down. At first, it was things like sporting events, concerts, parades, and then churches.

Sunday, March 15, was the first week that Abundant Life didn't assemble, because Pastor Phil wanted to follow the recommendation of our governing officials and practice "social distancing." Although I understood the reasoning, I was disappointed that I wasn't going to be sitting between my boys that day. I tried to look on the bright side and thought surely they would agree to attend church with me when I get baptized. Although that day wasn't yet planned, it was something to look forward to.

Within just one short week, more and more events were being cancelled. On a personal level, my TOPS Club got put on hold from headquarters until May 4th, as well as Planet Fitness closing their doors until further notice. I decided to send my chapter members weekly mailings to try and keep them motivated and would find other ways to exercise. With the onset of spring and nicer weather, I preferred walking outside anyway.

My dad, Kathy, BoBo, and I are huge *Survivor* fans. We like to make a big deal out of "Survivor Night," so every Wednesday we get together at my dad's house, and Kathy always makes a nice dinner. We even came up with a way to keep track of "tribe members" and who gets voted out each week. We decided it was probably best to put that on hold until after the coronavirus had simmered down.

One of the biggest impacts the coronavirus had on the community was school closings. Blue Springs Schools were supposed to resume classes after spring break. With the increasing threat, the Governor of

Missouri mandated that all classes were cancelled for the rest of the school year.

Carrie and Courtney are both elementary school teachers. Working in the district myself, I know on a personal level that this really impacted staff and students. When "goodbyes" were said before spring break, they fully expected to return the following week. And Brooklyn is a senior and didn't even get a chance for a proper farewell. She will never get the chance to walk the halls of high school again. The school year was cut short, and it affected everybody.

I thank God every day that I still had a job to go to. Being a custodian, it was our duty to make sure the building was deep cleaned and sanitized. Plus, there's always something to do to maintain a school, the job never ends.

The coronavirus closed a lot of local businesses all over the country. With the virus spreading, the only doors left open were basically grocery stores, drive-thru dining establishments, doctors' offices, and pharmacies. Everything that was considered "non-essential" was closed. Everybody was put on a lockdown and were expected to either go to work (if you still had a job to go to) or stay at home.

Isaiah and Hera just so happened to be among those affected by layoffs. This was beginning to be an economic crisis that was happening all over the world. It's a time of uncertainty and people were starting to freak out and hoard toilet paper (you know what I'm talking about).

Luckily Koen's job was secure since Cerner is in the healthcare industry. He did get a promotion within the company. Effective March 30th, he became a "change implementation analyst." He will be assigned and trained to a specific solution that they support and implement change requests in a live environment for clients.

Abundant Life had the capability to run a live stream for their services, so I was able to sit at home and view the worship team and hear Pastor Phil's sermon on my television through YouTube. It wasn't the same as gathering together as a congregation, but at least I didn't have to miss church altogether.

Pastor Phil took the opportunity through his message to let us know that with the coronavirus pandemic, God has surely gotten our attention. We need to be shaken loose of what we're bound to. In other words, all of our securities and idols. Our security has always been in our Lord Jesus Christ. It's never been in our money, jobs, entertainment, concerts, sporting events, etc.

Perhaps the coronavirus is God's way of purposely allowing this season to bring revival. It's time to stop, slow down, and really think about our values. Pastor Phil shared with his congregation that this is a time to be in prayerful preparation with a confidant expectation. 1 Thessalonians 5:16-18 tells us, "Be joyful always; pray continually; give thanks in all circumstances, for this is God's will for you in Christ Jesus." It's time for our country to ban together in peace and not live in fear.

Weeks three and four of our Next Steps classes had to be held online. Thank goodness for the capability of technology in times such as these. Week three was focused on serving. We learned that the lifeblood of Abundant Life is ministry and every member is a minister. That's how we demonstrate our love for people. There are a lot of opportunities to serve, and I'm looking forward to finding the best fit for me when we return to our church environment.

Week four focused on community and discipleship. Community is God's plan to shape us into His image. "As iron sharpens iron, so a man sharpens the countenance of his friend" (Proverbs 27:17). People need people, and at Abundant Life, community happens in groups to process life in Christ with one another.

Discipleship is a believer's personal ministry and calling. Growing people change, and if you're not changing, you're not learning. Pastor Phil says, "Every finish line is a new starting line." The goal of discipleship is reproduction. 2 Timothy 2:2: "And the things that you have heard from me among many witnesses, commit these to faithful men who will be able to teach others also." When the church ceases to make disciples, it ceases to exist.

Hanging out with Joe at the Santa Fe house proved to be a setback. Being there was a constant reminder that Joe could exist just fine without me. It was like ripping a Band-Aid off a wound before it could heal. I was able to shift my perspective and recognize that I no longer had the need to be there, that in time I was going to be just fine.

Furthermore, ceasing communication with him all together was a decision that had to be made. I thought I could be friends with Joe, but my heartstrings were still attached. If I thought letting go of our marriage was hard, letting go of our friendship was even harder. He wasn't a very good husband (he knows that), but he was a great friend. I knew that letting go and moving on meant walking away. I also knew I couldn't look back. I had a tear in my eye and an ache in my heart.

Psalm 91:14-16 comforts me, "Because he loves me," says the Lord, "I will rescue him; I will protect him, for he acknowledged my name. He will call upon me, and I will answer him; I will be with him in trouble, I will deliver him and honor him. With long life I will satisfy him and show him my salvation."

Once I began pursuing the Lord instead of pursuing Joe, I finally began to understand how to achieve true happiness.

I've always had low self-esteem and insecurities. I believe it roots back to my childhood where I was trying to earn my father's love. My dad doted on my younger sister, as I stood on the sidelines, waiting to be noticed, yearning for his attention.

As children, when we're most vulnerable, Satan starts whispering lies in our ears. He knows our weaknesses, and Satan made sure I grew up thinking I wasn't good enough, that I didn't measure up. When I got older, I didn't feel like I deserved to be loved, that love was something I had to earn. As an adult, I spent my married life trying to earn that love from my husband. All these years I thought my eating disorder was a way I controlled my empty emotions, but in reality, I wasn't controlling anything at all. I was actually spinning "out of control."

One of the many lessons I learned from Pastor Phil's teachings is that I am a Kingdom Warrior. That means that I have to put on the armor of God (Ephesians 6:10-17) and prepare for battle by <u>choosing</u> to live each day in spiritual victory. It was exactly that mentality that I used to turn from years of an eating disorder.

When I was able to look at bulimia as a sin, I was able to change my perspective. I wanted to claim victory over Satan. I no longer wanted him to have that stronghold on me, I refused to give him that much power over my life. I knew that I was a born-again child of God, and that I was perfectly created in His image. God is the great physician and my healer. He loves me, and it's time for me to love myself, for who I am.

Sin has many forms, and it's a stronghold that Satan has over all of us. I want you to know that no matter what stronghold you're held captive in, there is hope, and you can escape the bondage. It could be an addiction to drugs, alcohol, or food. Maybe it's sexual sin in the line of pornography or an immoral relationship. Abuse takes many forms as well, whether at the hands of another or your own. Or possibly, you suffer from a broken relationship, failed marriage, personal loss, depression, anxiety or an illness of any kind.

I just want you to know you can be set free by the blood of Jesus Christ. Acts 16:31 tells us, "Believe in the Lord Jesus, and you will be saved - you and your household." It's never too late to turn your life over to Jesus. He accepts you and loves you, just as you are.

2020 is not over yet, in fact it's just getting started. It's April and spring is in the air. Unfortunately, so is the coronavirus. It's still continuing to plague our nation. So much of our lives have changed and so much has been put on hold. We've definitely had to adapt. I'm looking forward to a time when we can resume some of the activities that we're all longing for.

Courtney's thirtieth birthday was April 3rd, and since we couldn't gather to celebrate, the family participated in a parade. Our line-up started on a side street where we decorated our cars with signs and balloons. My mom and Robert dressed as clowns and had their dogs, Jubi and Willow, with them. As we drove by her house, we tossed her gifts and cards (and rolls of toilet paper) and honked our horns. BoBo tailed the parade with colored paint cans while my nephew Gabe played "Happy Birthday" through the megaphone. The parade only lasted a few minutes, but to Courtney, the memory will last a lifetime.

As I mentioned in the introduction, this is a story of faith, hope, love and forgiveness. I would like to elaborate a little on what these words have come to mean to me over the years and in the course of my writing.

> FAITH: The bookmark in my Bible can always be found in Psalm 91. It's a beautiful passage of God's faithfulness. This is a fallen world that we live in full of evil, danger, and heartache. It's an uncertain time with the threat of illness, disease, and the coronavirus. In the midst of our most difficult days, God is our refuge and our fortress (v2), His faithfulness is our shield (v4), He will guard us in all our ways (v11), and He will be with us in trouble (v15). I challenge you to read this scripture, get to know it and hopefully you can draw comfort in difficult times, as I do.
>
> HOPE: The biblical definition of hope is the confident expectation of what God has promised and its strength is in His faithfulness. Romans 15:13 tells us, "May the God of hope fill you with all joy and peace as you trust in Him, so that you may overflow with hope by the power of the Holy Spirit." I chose "hope" for my word of the year for 2020.

If we put our hope in something, we're seeking something better. And I pray that whatever you're hoping for in this lifetime, you find it.

LOVE: 1 John 4:11: "Dear friends, since God so loved us, we also ought to love one another." Love is a choice, and it should never have to be earned. Just imagine if we all chose to love our spouses, parents, children, neighbors, and yes, even our enemies, this world could be a much brighter place. May you choose to love unconditionally and let your light shine.

FORGIVENESS: I have learned a lot about how to forgive, starting with myself. Years ago, when I made some very bad decisions, I hurt the people closest to me, my husband, and my kids. It took me a long time to finally be able to forgive myself. When Joe asked me if I could forgive him, I didn't hesitate. I've even learned how to forgive the woman that came between my husband and I. Colossians 3:13 tells us, "Bear with each other and forgive whatever grievances you may have against one another. Forgive as the Lord forgave you."

Offering forgiveness frees us to enjoy God's peace, restoring grace in all of our relationships and within ourselves. If we go around holding grudges and harboring angry, hateful feelings, we will become bitter human beings. Jesus paid the ultimate sacrifice by dying on the cross for our sins. Shouldn't we be able to forgive one another?

One Sunday when Abundant Life's teaching pastor, Chad Glover, was preaching, he made reference to looking forward to coming "home." He stated, when you pull up to your house, you're not thinking about the siding or the roof or the repairs that need to be done. You're thinking about what's inside, what's most important to you. Your family.

I chuckled when I heard that, because as much as I agree, I thought of Joe, because Joe is the one person I know that does indeed think about the siding on the house and the roof and all the repairs that need to be done as he pulls into his driveway. Unfortunately, Joe missed what was inside, what was really important, what should have mattered the most.

My favorite author of all times, Karen Kingsbury, New York Times Best Selling Christian Author, has about ninety titles she can claim, including e-short stories, children's titles, and gift books. I'm one of her biggest fans and have read over forty of her books (I still have a long way to go) and even got to meet her at a book signing once.

One of her titles, *A Time to Dance* was made into a movie, and I bought the DVD. I love the analogy that Corbin Bernsen's character quotes about marriage. He said, "A marriage is a house, you invest in it, you make the repairs, and you love it, because inside is everything that ever meant something to you." What a beautiful thought.

I can honestly say I've had a blessed and wonderful life and wouldn't change any of it. God never promised us a life free of trials and tribulations. In fact, He told us in this world, we will have trouble (John 16:33). I believe the storms I've personally gone through have made me a stronger woman and have made me who I am. The road had to be traveled to get to where I'm at today.

As I write these last few pages, I'm reminded of a DVR that catches up to real time. And as I sit in the stillness of my home and listen to the "tick-tock, tick-tock," of the clock, it tells me that, indeed, time continues to march on. This girl has a lot of life left to live. It may be the end of my book, but it's definitely not the end of my story...

Epilogue

I have been an avid journaler for years. Some say that journaling is very therapeutic, and I would tend to agree with that statement. There's something about jotting down thoughts, emotions, prayers, good times, sad times, special occasions, family events, holidays, etc. The list goes on and on. I had so much brewing inside of me that I couldn't contain it. I didn't even know the direction I was going, I just wanted to start putting my thoughts on paper. I told God that under no other circumstances, I wanted to glorify Him, so I asked Him to guide me and give me the words.

It was hard for me to walk away from twenty-five years with my husband. I never stopped loving Joe, but I learned how to love myself. When I was finally able to look at myself through the eyes of the Lord, I saw someone of value.

Out of the Darkness, Into the Light has come to mean so much more to me than a mere title. Darkness represents the sin in my life and the strongholds that Satan had me bound to. Light, of course, represents God and all His grace and mercy.

Galatians 5:16-26 speaks volumes to me. Verses 16 –18 says, "So I say, live by the Spirit, and you will not gratify the desires of the sinful nature. For the sinful nature desires what is contrary to the Spirit, and the Spirit what is contrary to the sinful nature. They are in conflict with each other, so that you do not do what you want. But if you are led by the Spirit, you are not under law."

Out of the "Darkness," represents Galatians 5:19-21: "The acts of the sinful nature are obvious: sexual immorality, impurity and debauchery; idolatry and witchcraft; hatred, discord, jealousy, fits of rage, selfish ambition, dissensions, factions, and envy; drunkenness, orgies, and the like. I warn you, as I did before, that those that live like this will not inherit the kingdom of God."

Into the "Light," represents Galatians 5:22-26: "But the fruit of the spirit is love, joy, peace, patience, kindness, goodness, faithfulness, gentleness and self-control. Against such things there is no law. Those who belong to Christ Jesus have crucified the sinful nature with its passions and desires. Since we live by the Spirit, let us keep in step with the Spirit. Let us not become conceited, provoking and envying each other."

The gift of salvation has already been given when Jesus Christ died on the cross for our sins. You don't have to earn it; you just have to accept it. So, won't you?

2012 Word for the Year

<u>Faithful</u>

~ Faithful to the Lord
~ Faithful to my Marriage
~ Faithful to my Relationships
~ Faithful to my Work and Seeking It
~ Faithful to my Diet and what I Eat
~ Faithful to my Exercise

"We live by faith, not by sight," 2 Corinthians 5:7

2013 Word for the Year

Contentment

Contentment comes in understanding that it is God who supplies our needs!

~ Content in knowing you Lord
~ Content in my Spouse and Kids
~ Content in my Job
~ Content in all You provide for me: health, shelter, clothing, food, and vehicle

> "And my God will meet all your needs according to His glorious riches in Christ Jesus," Phillipians 4:19

2014 Word for the Year

<u>Acceptance</u>

Accept each day, do not wish for different circumstances.

~ Accept myself for the unique person You created me to be
~ Accept Joe for who he is
~ Accept my children for who they are and who they become
~ Accept my circumstances
~ Accept where I'm at today, because it's exactly where You want me to be

> "And we know that in all things God works for the good of those who love Him, who have been called according to His purpose," Romans 8:28

2015 Word for the Year

<u>Confidence</u>

Freedom from doubt; belief in yourself and your abilities!

> "Do not throw away your confidence; it will be richly rewarded. You need to persevere so that when you have done the will of God, you will receive what he has promised," Hebrews 10:35-36

2016 Word for the Year

<u>Happiness</u>
A state of well-being and contentment; a pleasurable or satisfying experience.

Q: What makes someone happy?
A: Whatever it is they look forward to!

Happiness is a choice; we make our own weather.

2017 Word for the Year

Joy

The settled assurance that God is in control of the details of my life, the quiet confidence that ultimately everything is going to be alright, and the determined choice to praise God in every situation!

> "We're depending on God; He's everything we need. What's more, our hearts brim with joy since we've taken for our own His holy name," Psalm 33:20

2018 Word for the Year

Peace

Freedom from disturbance, tranquility, mental or emotional calm.

> "Now may the Lord of peace Himself give you peace at all times and in every way. The Lord be with all of you," 2 Thessalonians 3:16
>
> "The Lord gives strength to His people; the Lord blesses His people with peace," Psalm 29:11

2019 Word for the Year

Trust
Firm belief in the reliability, truth, ability, or strength of someone or something.

> "Trust in the Lord with all your heart, and lean not on your own understanding; in all your ways acknowledge Him, and He shall direct your paths," Proverbs 3:5-6

God, I know you'll provide for me financially as I step into this new chapter of my life. Where God leads He provides!

2020 Word for the Year

Hope

A confident expectation of something better!

> "May the God of hope fill you with all joy and peace as you trust in Him, so that you may overflow with hope by the power of the Holy Spirit," Romans 15:13

> "'For I know the plans I have for you,'" declares the Lord, "'plans to prosper you and not to harm you, plans to give you a hope and a future,'" Jeremiah 29:11

Narcissistic personality disorder

Also known as NPD

Symptoms

Being overly boastful, exaggerating one's own achievements
Pretending to be superior to others
Lack of empathy for others
Looking down on others as inferior
Monopolizing conversations
Impatient, angry, unhappy, depressed, or has mood swings
Easily disappointed when expected importance is not given
Always craves for "the best" in everything
Has a very fragile self-esteem

Causes

Exact causes are unknown, but may include:
Parenting style either excessive pampering or criticism
Genetic changes
Changes in the structure or functioning of brain

Prevention

Child abuse, both physical and mental and intimate partner abuse may be predisposing factors
Avoid domestic violence
Quit alcohol and smoking

Avoid drug abuse complications
Affects social relationships—at home, school, and/or office
Depression
Drug and/or alcohol abuse
Suicidal thoughts